Special Occasions in Cross-Stitch

Special Occasions in Cross-Stitch

WARM AND WELCOMING DESIGNS FOR HOLIDAYS AND CELEBRATIONS

By the Editors of Rodale Craft Books

Rodale Press, Emmaus, Pennsylvania

Our Mission

We publish books that empower people's lives.

RODALE BOOKS

Project designs and text by
Chapelle, Ltd., Ogden, UT 84401

Rodale Press
　　Executive Editor: Margaret Lydic Balitas
　　Crafts Editor: Suzanne Nelson
　　Craft Book Designer: Denise M. Shade
　　Copy Editor: Barbara M. Webb

If you have any questions or comments concerning this
book, please write:
　　Rodale Press
　　Book Readers' Service
　　33 East Minor Street
　　Emmaus, PA 18098

The cross-stitched border on the cover appears in Welcome
on page 148.

Library of Congress Cataloging-in-Publication Data

Special occasions in cross-stitch : warm and welcoming
　　designs for holidays and celebrations / by the editors of
　　Rodale craft books.
　　　　p.　　cm.
　　ISBN 0–87596–146–0　hardcover
　　1. Cross-stitch—Patterns.　2. Holiday decorations.
　I. Rodale Press.
　TT778.C76S64　1992
　746.44`3041–dc20
　　　　　　　　　　　　　　　　　92–14973
　　　　　　　　　　　　　　　　　CIP

NOTICE

The editors who compiled this book have tried to make all
of the contents as accurate and as correct as possible.
Graphs, illustrations, photographs, and text have all been
carefully checked and cross-checked. However, due to the
variability of local conditions, tools and supplies, personal
skill, and so on, Rodale Press assumes no responsibility for
any injuries suffered, or for damages or other losses
incurred, that result from the material presented herein. All
instructions should be carefully studied and clearly under-
stood before beginning a project.

Distributed in the book trade by St. Martin's Press

2　4　6　8　10　9　7　5　3　1　hardcover

Contents

Contents

A Year of Samplers

Welcome to a year full
of cross-stitch samplers!
Beginning with a snowman in
January (upper left corner),
stitch your way into
the images of summer
and right into a prism of color
in December's design.
The instructions for
these samplers
and patterns for
the wood cutouts
on each frame
appear throughout
the book.

Spring

Spring creeps in slowly, unfurling its soft and gentle colors one by one. With its arrival come so many glorious reasons to celebrate! This season, associated with fresh, new beginnings, brings us babies, bridal showers, Mother's Day and Easter. In this section, you'll find beautiful cross-stitched accents for your home and one-of-a-kind gift ideas. The abundant floral designs, with fresh green and soft pastels, borrow from Nature's springtime palette.

Spring Banner

Stitched on white Country Aida 7, the finished design size is 14" x 31½". The fabric was cut 20" x 45". See Suppliers for specialty thread and fabric.

Materials

Completed design on white Country Aida 7; matching thread
2½ yards of coordinating fabric; matching thread
1¼ yards of fleece
1¼ yards of fusible interfacing
2⅜ yards of large cording
16½" length of 1¼"-wide wooden closet rod
Two 1½" x 4½" wooden finials
Glue
Acrylic paints
Paintbrushes

Directions
All seams are ¼".

1. Trim design piece to 14½" x 39" with top edge of design 6½" from top edge of fabric. Cut a "V" in bottom edge of design piece; see **Diagram**. Using design piece as pattern, cut two fleece pieces and one piece from coordinating fabric for back. Also from coordinating fabric, cut 3"-wide bias strips, piecing as needed to equal 2⅜ yards. Make 2⅜ yards of corded piping.

2. Fuse interfacing to wrong side of design piece, following manufacturer's instructions. Pin fleece to wrong side of design piece. Zigzag edges. Press as needed to keep smooth. Stitch piping to front with right sides facing and raw edges aligned, rounding corners slightly. Clip corners and trim fleece from seam allowance.

3. With right sides facing, stitch front to back, sewing on stitching line of piping and leaving top short edge open for turning. Turn. Clean finish top short edge.

4. To make casing, fold top 3" to back and pin. Topstitch through all layers across top row of stitching on design.

5. Paint rod and finials with acrylic paints as desired. Allow to dry. Insert the rod in the casing. Glue a finial to each end of the rod.

Spring Banner

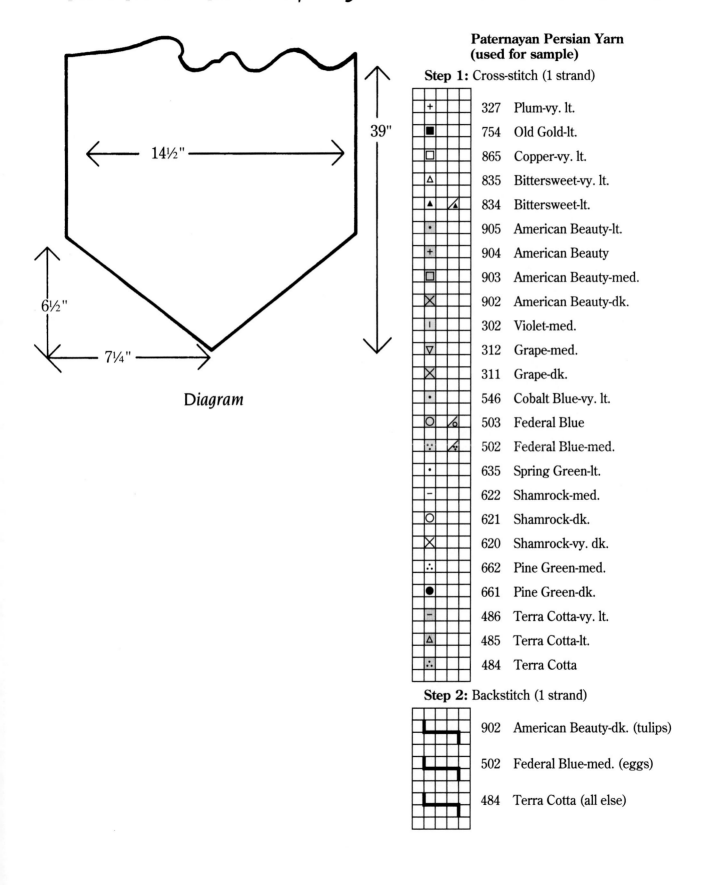

Diagram

14½"

39"

6½"

7¼"

Paternayan Persian Yarn (used for sample)

Step 1: Cross-stitch (1 strand)

Symbol		Number	Color
+		327	Plum-vy. lt.
■		754	Old Gold-lt.
□		865	Copper-vy. lt.
△		835	Bittersweet-vy. lt.
▲	◺	834	Bittersweet-lt.
▪		905	American Beauty-lt.
+		904	American Beauty
□		903	American Beauty-med.
⊠		902	American Beauty-dk.
ı		302	Violet-med.
▽		312	Grape-med.
⊠		311	Grape-dk.
•		546	Cobalt Blue-vy. lt.
○	◸	503	Federal Blue
∴	◿	502	Federal Blue-med.
•		635	Spring Green-lt.
–		622	Shamrock-med.
○		621	Shamrock-dk.
⊠		620	Shamrock-vy. dk.
∴		662	Pine Green-med.
●		661	Pine Green-dk.
⊟		486	Terra Cotta-vy. lt.
△		485	Terra Cotta-lt.
∴		484	Terra Cotta

Step 2: Backstitch (1 strand)

	Number	Color
	902	American Beauty-dk. (tulips)
	502	Federal Blue-med. (eggs)
	484	Terra Cotta (all else)

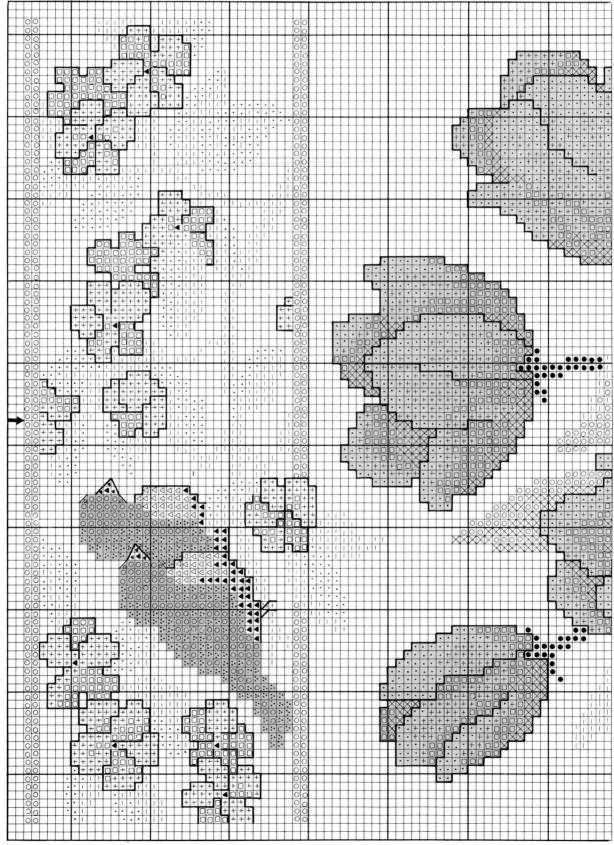

TOP

Spring Banner

TOP

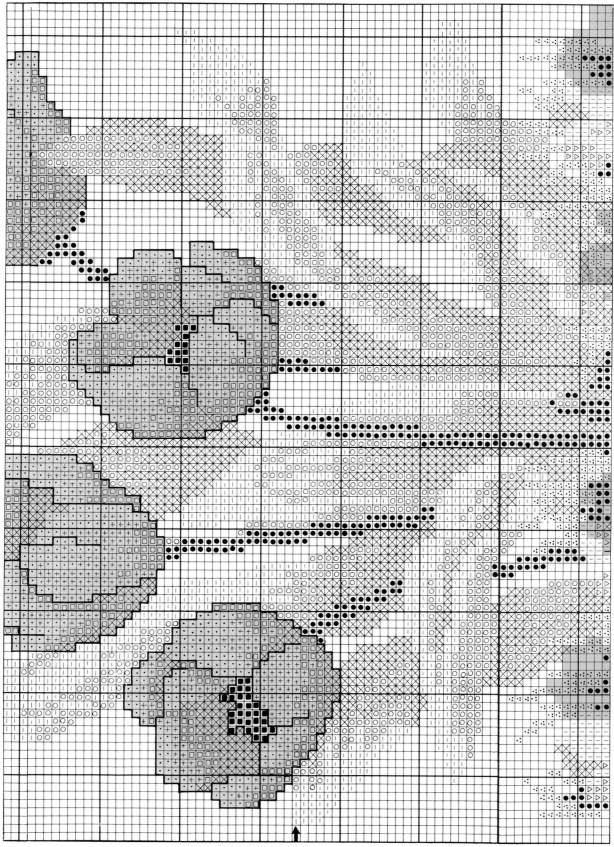

Spring Banner

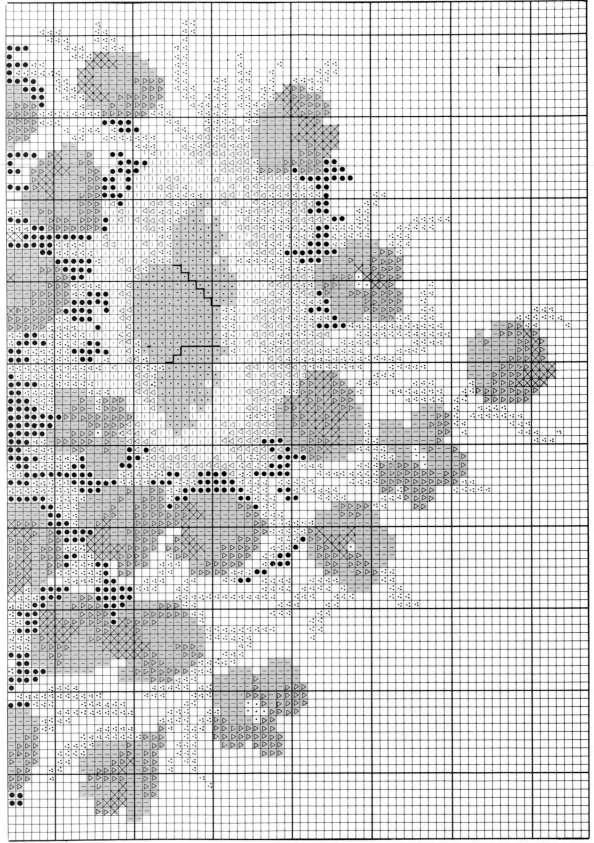

TOP

Stitch Count: 98 x 221

March Charm

March Charm

Stitched on cream Murano 30 over two threads, the finished design size is 4⅝" x 6⅝". The fabric was cut 11" x 13".

Directions

To complete, paint wood cutout (available at craft store or use pattern below) with acrylic paint as desired. Allow to dry. Center and glue a craft stick to back of cutout. Center and glue stick to back of frame.

March cutout

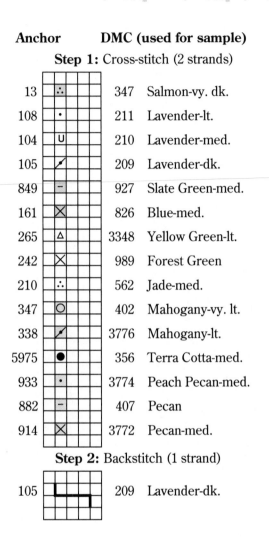

Anchor		DMC (used for sample)	
Step 1: Cross-stitch (2 strands)			
13	∴	347	Salmon-vy. dk.
108	·	211	Lavender-lt.
104	U	210	Lavender-med.
105	◤	209	Lavender-dk.
849	–	927	Slate Green-med.
161	✕	826	Blue-med.
265	△	3348	Yellow Green-lt.
242	✕	989	Forest Green
210	∴	562	Jade-med.
347	○	402	Mahogany-vy. lt.
338	◤	3776	Mahogany-lt.
5975	●	356	Terra Cotta-med.
933	·	3774	Peach Pecan-med.
882	–	407	Pecan
914	✕	3772	Pecan-med.
Step 2: Backstitch (1 strand)			
105	⌐	209	Lavender-dk.

Stitch Count: 70 x 100

Aunt Mary's Footstool

remove. Wrap fabric in a towel; press out excess solution. Let dry on flat surface. The fabric will dry a lighter shade than when wet. The irregular color pattern adds to the antique look. Paint footstool with acrylic paints as desired. Allow to dry.

3. Center and trim design piece to 14" x 12". Cut two 14" x 4" and two 4" x 19" strips of lavender fabric. Stitch 14" strips to 14" design edges. Stitch 19" strips to ends, overlapping 14" strips. Center and staple over insert; place in footstool.

Materials

Completed design on white Jobelan 28; matching thread
⅜ yard of lavender fabric; matching thread
Footstool (see Suppliers)
Acrylic paints
Paintbrushes
Sponges
Two black tea bags

Diagram 1   Diagram 2   Diagram 3

Directions

1. Graphs on pages 22 and 23 represent the two quarters of the lower half of design. First stitch Graph A, starting in center and placing design in lower right quarter (**Diagram 1**). Then stitch Graph B in lower left quarter (**Diagram 2**). Flip Graphs A and B, stitching the upper half as a mirror image; note that some symbols will be upside down (**Diagram 3**).

2. After stitching, tea-dye fabric for antique look, steeping tea bags in two cups of boiling water for five minutes. Remove bags; cool tea until tepid. Add four cups warm water; stir. Soak fabric for 10 minutes in solution;

Anchor			DMC (used for sample)	
			Step 1: Cross-stitch (2 strands)	
300	•		745	Yellow-lt. pale
301	-	⁄	744	Yellow-pale
4146	I		754	Peach-lt.
328	◄	⁄	3341	Apricot
49	∴		3689	Mauve-lt.
75	◁	⁄	604	Cranberry-lt.
28	●	⁄	3706	Melon-med.
108	✕		211	Lavender-lt.
104	◁	⁄	210	Lavender-med.
117	▢		3747	Blue Violet-vy. lt.
130	∴	⁄	809	Delft
213	-		369	Pistachio Green-vy. lt.
208	○		563	Jade-lt.
210	✕	⁄	562	Jade-med.

Aunt Mary's Footstool

TOP

HORIZONTAL CENTER OF DESIGN

VERTICAL CENTER OF DESIGN

GRAPH A

Aunt Mary's Footstool

VERTICAL CENTER OF DESIGN

Stitch Count: 182 x 154

GRAPH B

Country Pillow Pair

Rose and Green Pillow

Rose corner design: Stitched on ash rose Murano 30 over two threads, the finished design size is 2⅛" x 2⅛" for each motif. The fabric was cut 5" x 5" for each. Cut four, stitching one motif on each.

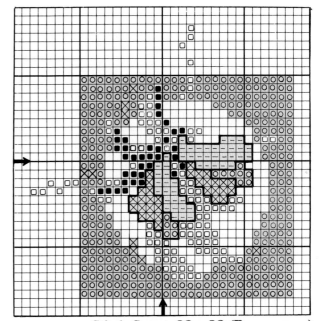

Stitch Count: 32 x 32 (Rose corner)

Anchor		DMC (used for sample)	

Step 1: Cross-stitch (2 strands)

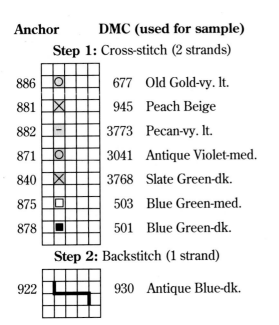

886	◯	677	Old Gold-vy. lt.
881	✕	945	Peach Beige
882	−	3773	Pecan-vy. lt.
871	◯	3041	Antique Violet-med.
840	✕	3768	Slate Green-dk.
875	☐	503	Blue Green-med.
878	■	501	Blue Green-dk.

Step 2: Backstitch (1 strand)

| 922 | | 930 | Antique Blue-dk. |

Materials
(for one pillow)

Completed center design on moss green or ash rose Murano 30; matching thread

Four completed corner designs on ash rose or pewter Murano 30; matching thread

1¼ yards of print fabric

1 yard of green pin dot fabric; matching thread

⅜ yard of floral print fabric

⅛ yard of light green fabric

⅛ yard of gold fabric; matching thread

Scrap of purple or dark green fabric

Two 16" squares of fleece

16" square of muslin

1¾ yards of medium cording

Dressmaker's pen

Polyester stuffing

reen center design: Stitched on moss green Murano 30 over two threads, the finished design size is 6⅞" x 6¾". The fabric was cut 10" x 10". Center design and begin stitching.

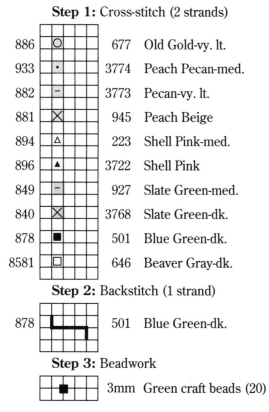

Anchor		DMC	(used for sample)

Step 1: Cross-stitch (2 strands)

886	◯	677	Old Gold-vy. lt.
933	·	3774	Peach Pecan-med.
882	−	3773	Pecan-vy. lt.
881	✕	945	Peach Beige
894	△	223	Shell Pink-med.
896	▲	3722	Shell Pink
849	−	927	Slate Green-med.
840	✕	3768	Slate Green-dk.
878	■	501	Blue Green-dk.
8581	☐	646	Beaver Gray-dk.

Step 2: Backstitch (1 strand)

| 878 | | 501 | Blue Green-dk. |

Step 3: Beadwork

| | ■ | 3mm | Green craft beads (20) |

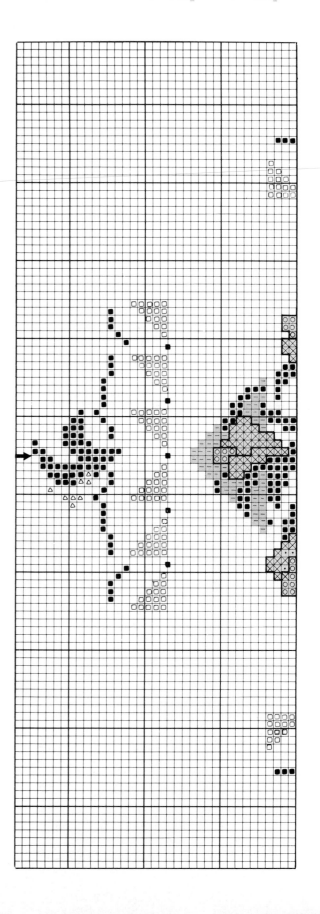

Country Pillow Pair

Stitch Count: 103 x 102 (Green center)

Country Pillow Pair

Directions
(for one pillow)
All seams are ¼".

1. Center and trim center design to 8" square. Center and trim corner designs to 3" square. From gold fabric, cut four 9" x 1½" strips. From purple or dark green fabric, cut four templates. From light green fabric, cut four 11¼" x 1¾" strips. From pin dot fabric, cut one 16" square back and 4"-wide border strips, piecing to equal 3½ yards. From floral print, cut 1¾"-wide bias strips, piecing to equal 1¾ yards for corded piping. From print fabric, cut 9"-wide bias ruffle strips, piecing to equal 5 yards.

2. Fold seam allowance under on two inside corner design edges. Place one corner design in each corner of center design; see photo. Slipstitch inside edges.

3. Stitch one gold strip to center design with right sides facing and long raw edges aligned, leaving 2" unstitched at bottom (**Diagram 1**). Stitch remaining strips (**Diagram 2**). Finish stitching first strip.

4. Fold under long edge of each Template. Place one on right side of gold strips at each corner, slipstitching long edge in place.

5. Repeat Step 3 with light green strips (**Diagram 3**).

6. Join border pieces end-to-end. Sew gathering threads on both long edges. Fold long edges into quarters and mark, matching to corners. Gather one edge to fit light green edges, allowing extra fullness at each corner. Stitch with right sides facing.

7. Layer muslin, one fleece piece and bordered design square, right side up. Baste. Gather remaining border edge to lie smoothly. Baste border to muslin. Trim to match muslin edges. Stitch cording to border edge, right sides facing and raw edges aligned.

8. Join ruffle piece end-to-end. Fold with wrong sides facing into a 4½"-wide strip; press. Sew gathering threads through both layers. Fold into quarters and mark raw edge, matching to bordered design square corners. Gather ruffle to fit, allowing extra fullness at each corner. Stitch on piping stitching line.

9. With matching thread, quilt around center design, on inside seam around green border, in-the-ditch around the two inside edges of each corner design, around each stitched design in corner design squares and in-the-ditch around edge of center design. With gold thread, quilt inside seam around gold border and in-the-ditch on outside seam around each Template/gold border.

10. Pin remaining fleece to wrong side of back. Zigzag edges. Press to keep smooth. Stitch bordered design square to back with right sides facing. Stitch on ruffle stitching line, leaving an opening. Clip corners. Turn. Stuff pillow firmly. Slipstitch opening closed.

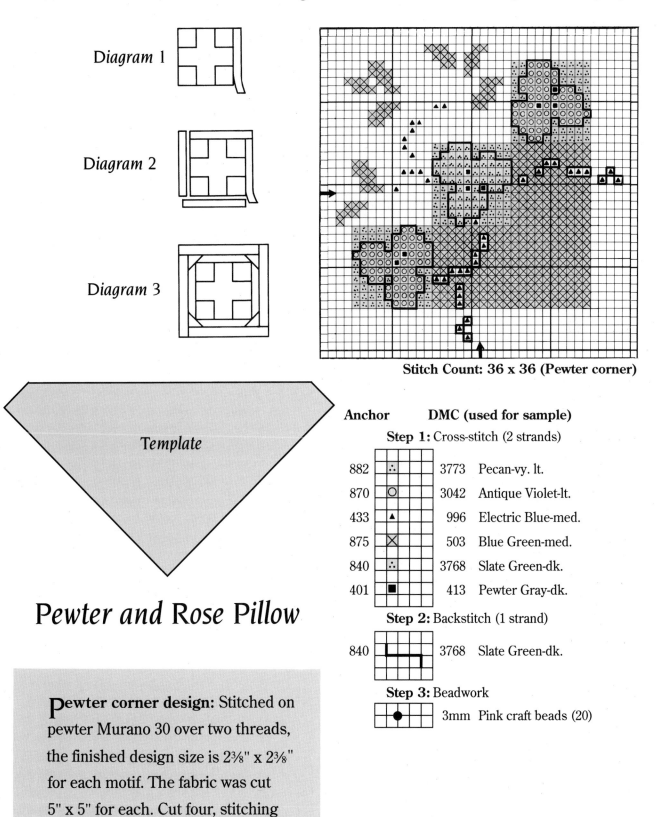

Diagram 1

Diagram 2

Diagram 3

Stitch Count: 36 x 36 (Pewter corner)

Template

Pewter and Rose Pillow

Pewter corner design: Stitched on pewter Murano 30 over two threads, the finished design size is 2⅜" x 2⅜" for each motif. The fabric was cut 5" x 5" for each. Cut four, stitching one motif on each.

Anchor		DMC (used for sample)	

Step 1: Cross-stitch (2 strands)

Anchor		DMC	
882	∴	3773	Pecan-vy. lt.
870	○	3042	Antique Violet-lt.
433	▲	996	Electric Blue-med.
875	✕	503	Blue Green-med.
840	∴	3768	Slate Green-dk.
401	■	413	Pewter Gray-dk.

Step 2: Backstitch (1 strand)

840		3768	Slate Green-dk.

Step 3: Beadwork

●	3mm	Pink craft beads (20)

Country Pillow Pair

Rose center design: Stitched on ash rose Murano 30 over two threads, the finished design size is 7⅛" x 7⅛". The fabric was cut 11" x 11". Center design and begin stitching.

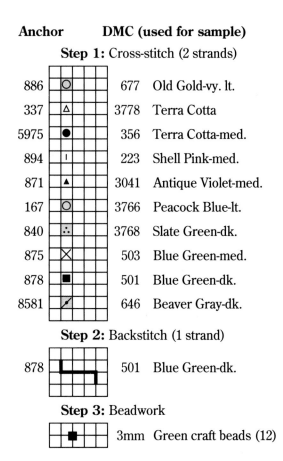

Anchor		DMC (used for sample)	

Step 1: Cross-stitch (2 strands)

Anchor		DMC	
886	○	677	Old Gold-vy. lt.
337	△	3778	Terra Cotta
5975	●	356	Terra Cotta-med.
894	ı	223	Shell Pink-med.
871	▲	3041	Antique Violet-med.
167	◎	3766	Peacock Blue-lt.
840	∴	3768	Slate Green-dk.
875	✕	503	Blue Green-med.
878	■	501	Blue Green-dk.
8581	╱	646	Beaver Gray-dk.

Step 2: Backstitch (1 strand)

878		501	Blue Green-dk.

Step 3: Beadwork

		3mm	Green craft beads (12)

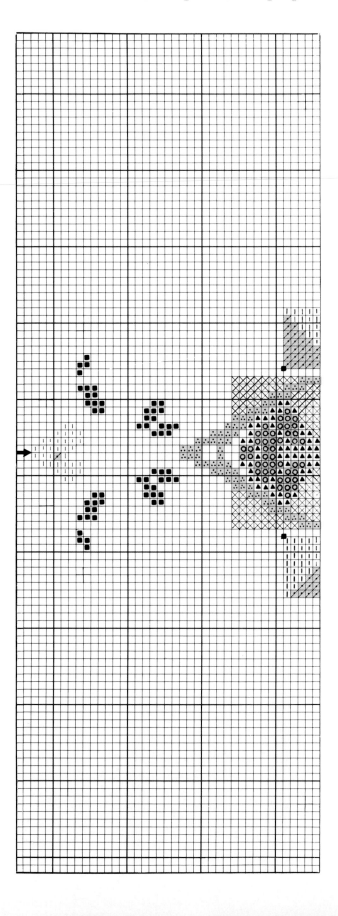

Country Pillow Pair

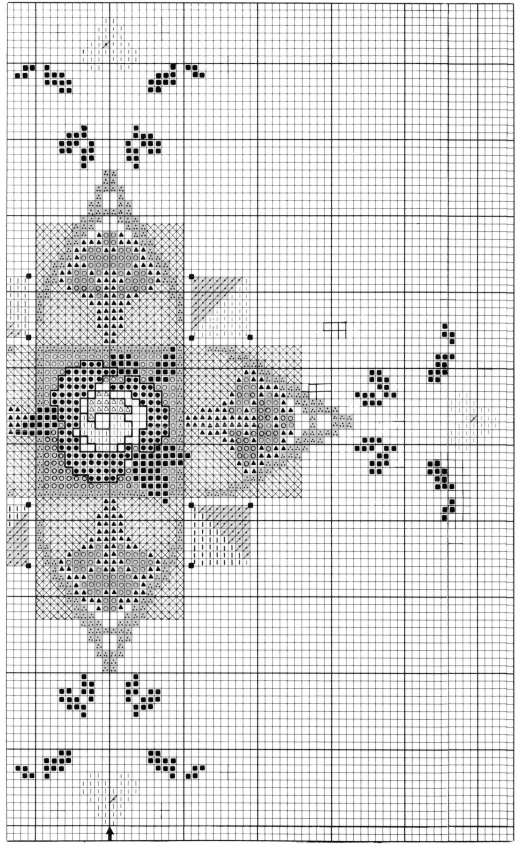

Stitch Count: 106 x 106 (Rose center)

April "Egg"stasy

Stitched on Wedgwood Murano 30 over two threads, the finished design size is 4⅝" x 6¼". The fabric was cut 11" x 13". See March Charm on page 18 for cutout instructions. More than one thread represented by a single symbol on the code and graph indicates blending; note the number of strands used.

April cutout

Anchor		DMC (used for sample)	
	Step 1: Cross-stitch (2 strands)		
1	· /		White
300	I	745	Yellow-lt. pale
301	□	744	Yellow-pale
4146	■ ◪	754	Peach-lt.
48	·	818	Baby Pink
300 / 24	□	<745 / 776	Yellow-lt. pale (1 strand)+ Pink-med. (1 strand)
24	△	776	Pink-med.
76	✕	962	Wild Rose-med.
108	○	211	Lavender-lt.
104	∴	210	Lavender-med.
158	⊠	775	Baby Blue-vy. lt.
203	○	954	Nile Green
204	●	912	Emerald Green-lt.
208	–	563	Jade-lt.
210	△	562	Jade-med.
212	▲	561	Jade-vy. dk.
378	+	841	Beige Brown-lt.
380	∴ ◿	839	Beige Brown-dk.
397 / 398	– ╱	<762 / 415	Pearl Gray-vy. lt. (1 strand) Pearl Gray (1 strand)
399	○	318	Steel Gray-lt.
400	✕	414	Steel Gray-dk.
	Step 2: Backstitch (1 strand)		
401	⌐	413	Pewter Gray-dk.

April "Egg"stasy

Stitch Count: 70 x 94

Mr. Fancy Pants

Mr. Fancy Pants

Stitched on khaki Linda 27 over two threads, the finished design size is 1" x 4½" for each motif. The fabric was cut 16" x 8". Stitch motifs to fill fabric. Heavy lines on graph indicate placement of additional motifs.

Materials

Completed design on khaki Linda 27; matching thread
6½" x 11½" piece of pink ultra suede fabric
4" x 7" piece of unbleached muslin
5½" x 9" piece of tan ultra suede fabric
10" x 10" piece of green baby checked fabric
8" x 14" piece of brown fabric
16" x 16" piece of fusible interfacing
Five ¼"-wide green buttons; matching thread
⅝ yard of ¼"-wide green satin ribbon
⅜ yard of ¼"-wide brown satin ribbon
Acrylic paints: brown, white and peach
Black permanent fine-tip marker
Gold stud
Polyester stuffing
Sand
Tracing paper
Dressmaker's pen

Directions

All seams are ¼".

1. Trace patterns and cut two pant pieces each from design piece and interfacing, positioning pattern ½" above first row of stitching. From pink suede, cut two heads, two ears and two paws. From muslin, cut two ears and two paws. From tan suede, cut two bags and two 9" x ½" pieces, one each for handle and belt. Cut two 5" squares for sleeves and one 9¾" x 4½" piece for shirt, each from checked fabric and fusible interfacing. Cut two boot sides, two boot backs and two soles, each from brown fabric and interfacing. Cut green ribbon into one 9" and four 3" lengths.

2. Fuse interfacing to wrong side of pants, sleeves, shirt and boot pieces, following manufacturer's instructions.

3. With right sides facing and raw edges aligned, stitch each boot side to each boot back, leaving inseam open. With right sides facing, stitch pant pieces together, leaving inseam open. Sew gathering threads along each pant leg bottom; gather to fit boot tops. With right sides facing, stitch each boot top to each gathered pant leg. Close pant and boot inseam. With right sides facing, stitch soles to boots. Turn. Set aside.

4. Mark vertical center of shirt. Sew buttons ¼" apart on right side of fabric, beginning ¾" from one raw edge. With right sides facing and short raw edges aligned, stitch shirt together. With right sides facing, stitch one raw edge of shirt to pant waist. Fold

remaining raw edge ¼" double to wrong side and stitch, forming a casing. Turn. Insert a 9" green ribbon length in casing. Set aside.

5. With right sides facing and raw edges aligned, sew each sleeve together. Fold each end ¼" double to wrong side, forming a casing. Insert a 3" green ribbon length in each casing. Set aside.

6. With right sides facing and raw edges aligned, sew head pieces together, leaving short straight edge open. Turn. Stuff firmly. Paint face according to pattern, outlining fine lines with marker.

7. Line ear with muslin, topstitching around outer edge for support. With right sides facing, stitch ear together going up ½" from bottom. Turn. Slipstitch bottom of ear to top of head. Repeat with remaining ear. Paint muslin on each ear with a pink wash.

8. With wrong sides facing, topstitch muslin to pink suede paw, leaving short end open. Stuff firmly. Repeat with remaining paw.

9. Fill boots and half way up pants with sand. Stuff remainder of pants and shirt. Insert head into shirt. Pull ribbon at neck to fit head and knot. Slipstitch neck to shirt.

10. Pull ribbon to gather one end of sleeve and knot. Slipstitch end at shoulder of shirt. Stuff sleeve. Insert paw into sleeve. Pull ribbon to fit paw and knot. Slipstitch paw to sleeve. Repeat with remaining sleeve and paw.

11. With right sides facing and raw edges aligned, stitch bag pieces together, leaving short straight edge open. Center wrong side of each handle end over right side of seam and tack. Tack center of handle to one shoulder of rabbit.

12. Mark center of belt piece and attach stud. Wrap belt around waist. Tack ends at back.

13. Wrap brown ribbon around rabbit's neck, tying a bow in front.

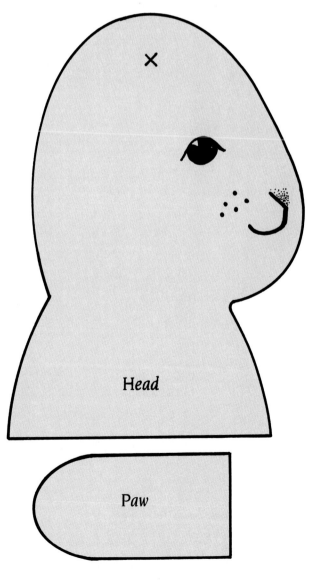

Head

Paw

Mr. Fancy Pants

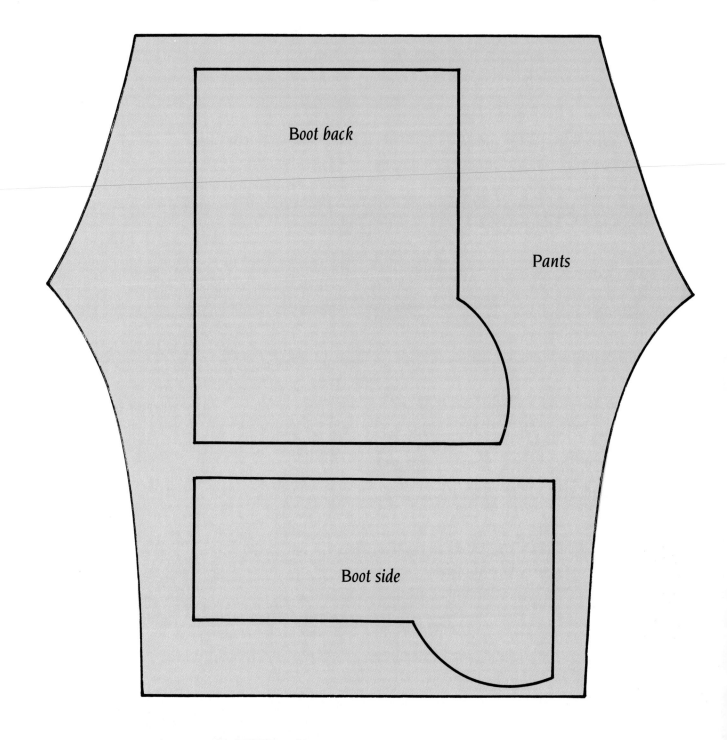

Boot back

Pants

Boot side

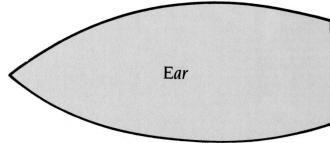

Ear

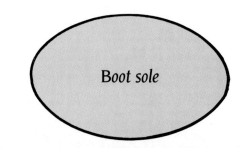

Boot sole

Mr. Fancy Pants

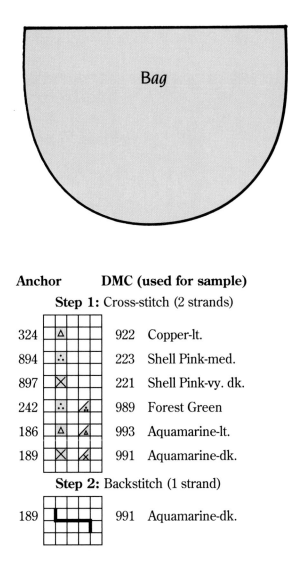

Bag

Anchor   **DMC (used for sample)**

Step 1: Cross-stitch (2 strands)

324	△	922	Copper-lt.
894	∴	223	Shell Pink-med.
897	✕	221	Shell Pink-vy. dk.
242	∴ ◿	989	Forest Green
186	△ ◸	993	Aquamarine-lt.
189	✕ ◹	991	Aquamarine-dk.

Step 2: Backstitch (1 strand)

| 189 | | 991 | Aquamarine-dk. |

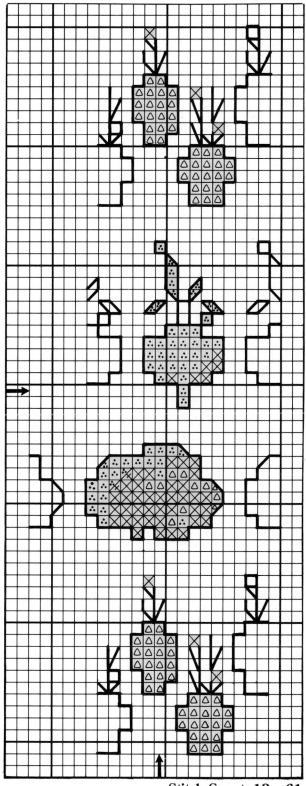

Stitch Count: 13 x 61

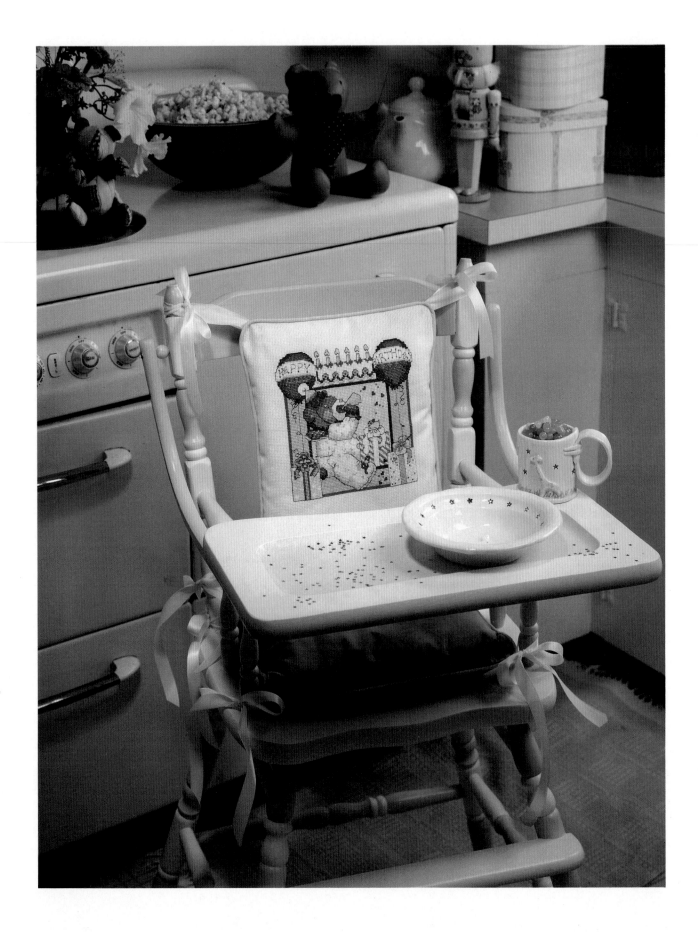

Happy Birthday, Baby

Stitched on white Aida 14, the finished design size is 6⅞" x 6⅞". See Step 1 of Directions before cutting and stitching fabric.

Materials

Completed design on white Aida 14
⅜ yard of light blue fabric; matching
  thread
⅜ yard of light green fabric
⅜ yard of light yellow fabric; matching
  thread
1 yard of batting
8 yards of ⅝"-wide white ribbon
2½ yards of medium cording
High chair

Directions

All seams are ¼".

1. Measure seat and back of high chair. Cut one piece each of blue and green fabric to the seat measurements. Cut one piece of blue fabric to the back measurements. Cut the design piece to match the back plus 2", centering the design with an equal distance for side and top borders. Cut four layers of batting for both the seat and back.

2. From yellow fabric, cut 1¾"-wide bias strips, piecing as needed to measure the distance around the outside edges of the seat and back. Make corded piping. Cut eight 1-yard ribbon lengths. Fold ribbon lengths in half, and pin folds in place. Set aside.

3. Stitch piping to design piece with right sides facing and raw edges aligned, rounding corners slightly. Pin the fold of one ribbon at the corner with the tails toward the inside and the fold on the raw edge of the design piece. Repeat at each corner. With right sides together, stitch the design piece and the blue fabric on the stitching line of the piping, catching the fold of the ribbons in the seams and leaving a 5" opening in one edge. Turn. Stuff with four batting layers. Slipstitch opening closed. Repeat to make seat.

Happy Birthday, Baby

Anchor **DMC (used for sample)**

Step 1: Cross-stitch (2 strands)

Anchor			DMC	
1	·	╱		White
297	∴	╱	743	Yellow-med.
303	◇		742	Tangerine-lt.
48	–	╱	818	Baby Pink
25	○	╱	3326	Rose-lt.
42	✕	╱	335	Rose
59	●	╱	326	Rose-vy. dk.
159		╱	827	Blue-vy. lt.
168	△	╱	807	Peacock Blue
169	■		806	Peacock Blue-dk.
205	I		911	Emerald Green-med.
229	▽	╱	909	Emerald Green-vy. dk.
189	✕	╱	991	Aquamarine-dk.
378	▢	╱	841	Beige Brown-lt.
379	∴	╱	840	Beige Brown-med.
380	▲	╱	839	Beige Brown-dk.
397	U	U	762	Pearl Gray-vy. lt.
398	K		415	Pearl Gray

Step 2: Backstitch (1 strand)

Anchor		DMC	
25	⌐	3326	Rose-lt. (stripes on white present)
189	⌐	991	Aquamarine-dk. (lettering)
382	⌐	3371	Black Brown (all else)

Step 3: French Knot (1 strand)

Anchor		DMC	
25	●	3326	Rose-lt.
189	◆	991	Aquamarine-dk.
382	▼	3371	Black Brown

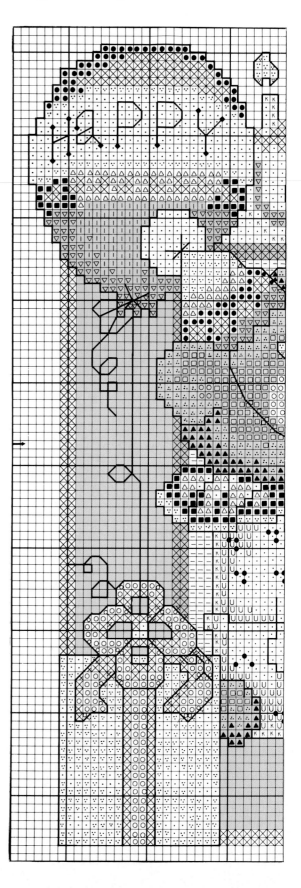

Happy Birthday, Baby

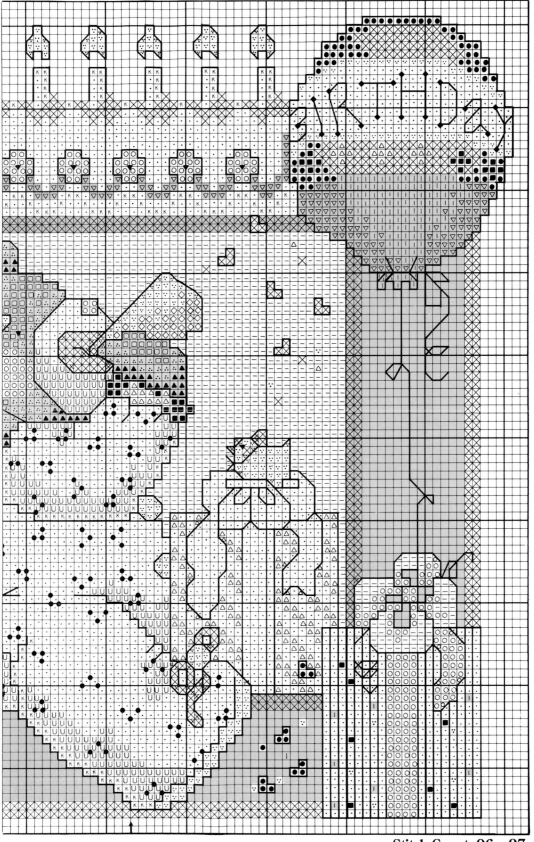

Stitch Count: 96 x 97

Bushel of Love

Stitched on Wedgwood Murano 30 over two threads, the finished design size is 5¼" x 2⅛" for each motif. See Steps 1–2 of Directions before cutting and stitching fabric. More than one thread represented by a single symbol on the code and graph indicates blending; note the number of strands used.

Materials

Completed design on Wedgwood Murano 30; matching thread
Basket

Directions

All seams are ¼".

1. Before stitching design, measure around basket where placement is desired and add 6" to establish horizontal measurement. Add 6" to vertical measurement of motif. Cut unstitched fabric to match measurements.

2. Center design vertically; begin stitching first motif 3" from one short end of fabric. Stitch motifs to fill horizontal measurement, leaving 3" unstitched at opposite end. Heavy lines on graph indicate placement of additional motifs. Measure 1½" above and below design; trim fabric. Trim 2½" from each short end.

3. With right sides facing, fold design in half lengthwise. Stitch long edge to make a tube. Turn right side out. Position seam in center back and press.

4. Fold in seam allowance on one end of band. Wrap band around basket. Insert raw edge of other end into folded end. Slipstitch ends together.

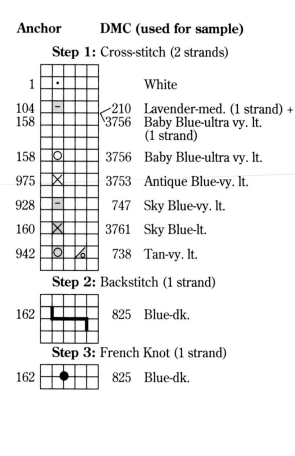

Anchor   DMC (used for sample)

Step 1: Cross-stitch (2 strands)

1	·	White
104	−	⟨210 Lavender-med. (1 strand) +
158		⟨3756 Baby Blue-ultra vy. lt. (1 strand)
158	O	3756 Baby Blue-ultra vy. lt.
975	X	3753 Antique Blue-vy. lt.
928	−	747 Sky Blue-vy. lt.
160	X	3761 Sky Blue-lt.
942	O ╱	738 Tan-vy. lt.

Step 2: Backstitch (1 strand)

162	⌐	825 Blue-dk.

Step 3: French Knot (1 strand)

162	●	825 Blue-dk.

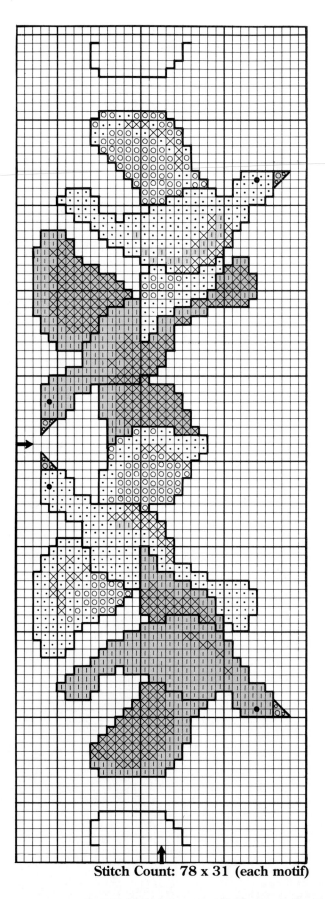

Stitch Count: 78 x 31 (each motif)

Easter Bands

Basket Band

Stitched on white Linda 27 over two threads, the finished design size is 1" x 2⅛" for each motif. See Steps 1–2 of Directions before cutting and stitching fabric.

Materials

Completed design on white Linda 27;
  matching thread
Basket

Directions
All seams are ¼".

1. Before stitching design, measure around basket where placement is desired and add 6" for horizontal measurement. Add 6" to vertical measurement of motif. Cut unstitched fabric to match measurements.

2. Center design vertically and begin stitching first motif 2½" from one short end of fabric. Stitch motifs to fill horizontal measurement, leaving 2½" unstitched at opposite end. Heavy lines on graph indicate placement of additional motifs. Measure 1¼" above and below design; trim fabric. Trim 2¼" from each short end.

3. With right sides facing, fold design in half lengthwise. Stitch long edge to make a tube. Turn right side out. Position seam in center back and press.

4. Fold in seam allowance on one end of band. Wrap band around basket. Insert raw edge of other end into folded end, making design meet. Slipstitch ends together.

Narrow Band

Stitched on white Linda 27 over two threads, the finished design size is 1" x ½" for each motif. See Steps 2-3 of Directions on page 49 before cutting and stitching fabric.

Materials

Completed design on white Linda 27;
  matching thread
Wooden egg or miniature wire bird cage
Acrylic paints
Paintbrushes
Sponges

Easter Bands

Directions

All seams are ¼".

1. Paint egg or bird cage with acrylic paints as desired. Allow to dry.

2. Before stitching design, measure around egg or bird cage and add 3" for horizontal measurement. Add 3" to vertical measurement of motif. Cut unstitched fabric to match measurements.

3. Choose one horizontal design pair; center vertically. Stitch first motif 1¼" from one short end of fabric. Stitch motifs to fill horizontal measurement, leaving 1¼" unstitched at opposite end. Heavy lines on graph indicate placement of additional motifs. Measure ⅝" above and below design; trim fabric. Trim 1¼" from each short end.

4. With right sides facing, fold design in half lengthwise. Stitch long edge to make a tube. Turn right side out. Position seam in center back and press.

5. Fold in seam allowance on one end of band. Wrap band around egg or bird cage. Insert raw edge of other end into folded end. Slipstitch ends together.

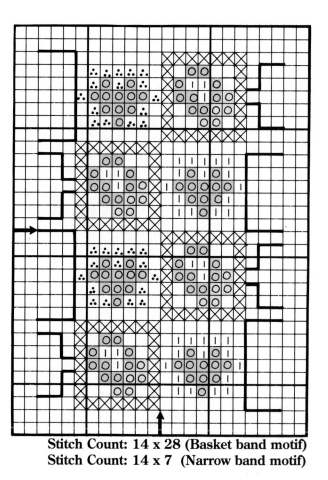

Stitch Count: 14 x 28 (Basket band motif)
Stitch Count: 14 x 7 (Narrow band motif)

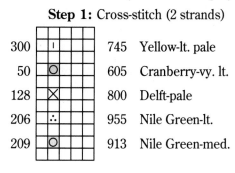

Anchor		DMC (used for sample)	
		Step 1: Cross-stitch (2 strands)	
300	ꞁ	745	Yellow-lt. pale
50	O	605	Cranberry-vy. lt.
128	X	800	Delft-pale
206	∴	955	Nile Green-lt.
209	O	913	Nile Green-med.

May Days

Stitched on white Linda 27 over two threads, the finished design size is 5¼" x 7⅜". The fabric was cut 12" x 14". See March Charm on page 18 for cutout instructions.

May cutout

Anchor			DMC	(used for sample)

Step 1: Cross-stitch (2 strands)

Anchor			DMC	
778	I	⁄	948	Peach-vy. lt.
8	△	⁄	353	Peach
10	●	⁄	352	Coral-lt.
24	–		776	Pink-med.
27	⁄		899	Rose-med.
49	·	⁄	3689	Mauve-lt.
66	○	⁄	3688	Mauve-med.
69	✕	⁄	3687	Mauve
108	–		211	Lavender-lt.
104	△		210	Lavender-med.
158	–		775	Baby Blue-vy. lt.
121	∴	⁄	793	Cornflower Blue-med.
214	□	⁄	966	Baby Green-med.
215	∴		320	Pistachio Green-med.
882	✕		407	Pecan

Step 2: Backstitch (1 strand)

Anchor		DMC	
11		351	Coral (peach flowers)
69		3687	Mauve (mauve flowers)
940		792	Cornflower Blue-dk. (lettering)
215		320	Pistachio Green-med. (all else)

Stitch Count: 70 x 100

Bath Towels

Bath Towels

Stitched on pistachio Pastel Linen 28 over two threads, the finished design size is 3½" x 3¾" for each motif. See Steps 1-2 of Directions before cutting and stitching.

Materials

Completed design on pistachio Pastel Linen 28; matching thread
1 yard of turquoise polyester lining fabric; matching thread
2½ yards of small cording
Towel

Directions
All seams are ¼".

1. Measure towel width where placement is desired and add 6" for measurement. The vertical measurement is 7". Cut unstitched linen to match measurements.

2. Center and stitch first motif, repeating as desired. Heavy lines on graph indicate placement of additional motifs. Measure 1⅝" above and below design; trim fabric. Trim 2½" from each short end.

3. From lining, cut 7"-wide strips, piecing as needed to equal three times the width measurement. Also cut 1"-wide bias strips as needed to equal two times the width measurement; make corded piping. Cut piping into two equal lengths. Stitch one length to each long edge of design; trim.

4. Hem one long edge of lining strip. Pin pleats ½" deep and ½" apart on remaining long raw edge to match width measurement of towel; baste. Steam press.

5. With right sides facing, stitch pleats to long edge of design on stitching line of piping. Trim edges of pleating, but do not unfold. On right side of towel, place wrong side of pleats ½" above short hemmed end of towel. Stitch through all layers on stitching line of piping. Unfold wrong side of design over right side of towel; press. Fold under seam allowance on remaining long edge of design. Stitch in-the-ditch of piping. Hem short edges of design and pleats.

Bath Towels

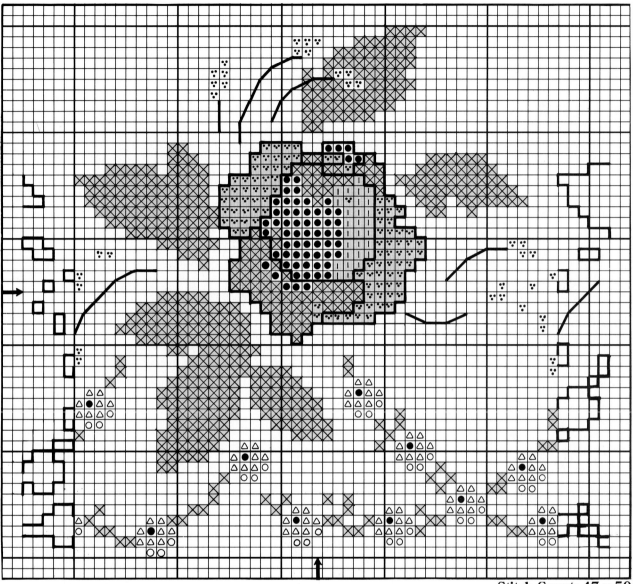

Stitch Count: 47 x 50

Anchor   **DMC (used for sample)**

Step 1: Cross-stitch (2 strands)

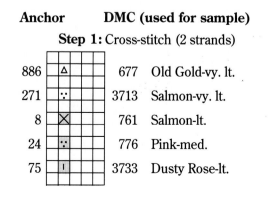

886	△	677	Old Gold-vy. lt.
271	∴	3713	Salmon-vy. lt.
8	✕	761	Salmon-lt.
24	∴	776	Pink-med.
75	ı	3733	Dusty Rose-lt.

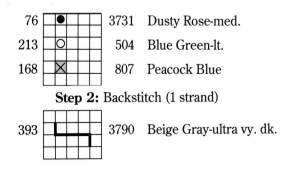

76	●	3731	Dusty Rose-med.
213	○	504	Blue Green-lt.
168	✕	807	Peacock Blue

Step 2: Backstitch (1 strand)

| 393 | | 3790 | Beige Gray-ultra vy. dk. |

Vanity Set

Dresser Scarf

Stitched on driftwood Belfast Linen 32 over two threads, the finished design size is 6¼" x 5". The fabric was cut 14" x 57". More than one thread represented by a single symbol on the code and graph indicates blending; note the number of strands used.

Materials

Completed design on driftwood Belfast
  Linen 32; matching thread
1¼ yards of pink braid
½ yard of blue braid
Dressmaker's pen

Directions

1. For tasseled ends, measure and mark 3½"–4" from each short raw edge. Begin pulling horizontal threads in fabric below marks. Secure by knotting five unraveled threads against first row of unpulled threads; continue horizontally forming fringe. Trim to 3".

2. To hem, measure and mark ½" from each long raw edge of design piece. Pull one thread, following marks. Crease along line formed by pulled threads, folding ¼" double to wrong side of fabric; hem.

3. Cut pink braid into three equal lengths. Slipstitch one length 1" from and parallel to fringe knots. Stitch each remaining braid ¼" apart in the following order: blue, pink, pink; see photo.

Anchor		DMC (used for sample)	
Step 1: Cross-stitch (2 strands)			
868	U	3779	Terra Cotta-vy. lt.
337	▲	3778	Terra Cotta
892	I	225	Shell Pink-vy. lt.
893	+	224	Shell Pink-lt.
893 894	□	224 223	Shell Pink-lt. (1 strand)+ Shell Pink-med. (1 strand)
894	✕	223	Shell Pink-med.
968	O	778	Antique Mauve-vy. lt.
870	▽	3042	Antique Violet-lt.
871	∴	3041	Antique Violet-med.
975	I	3753	Antique Blue-vy. lt.
920	△	932	Antique Blue-lt.
779	∴	926	Slate Green
842	□	3013	Khaki Green-lt.
875	∴	503	Blue Green-med.
876	●	502	Blue Green
858	–	524	Fern Green-vy. lt.
860	O	523	Fern Green-lt.
859 862	✕	522 520	Fern Green (1 strand)+ Fern Green-dk. (1 strand)
892 885	·	225 739	Shell Pink-vy. lt. (1 strand)+ Tan-ultra vy. lt. (1 strand)
885	⁒	739	Tan-ultra vy. lt.
942	✕	738	Tan-vy. lt.
379	⁄	840	Beige Brown-med.
380	■	839	Beige Brown-dk.

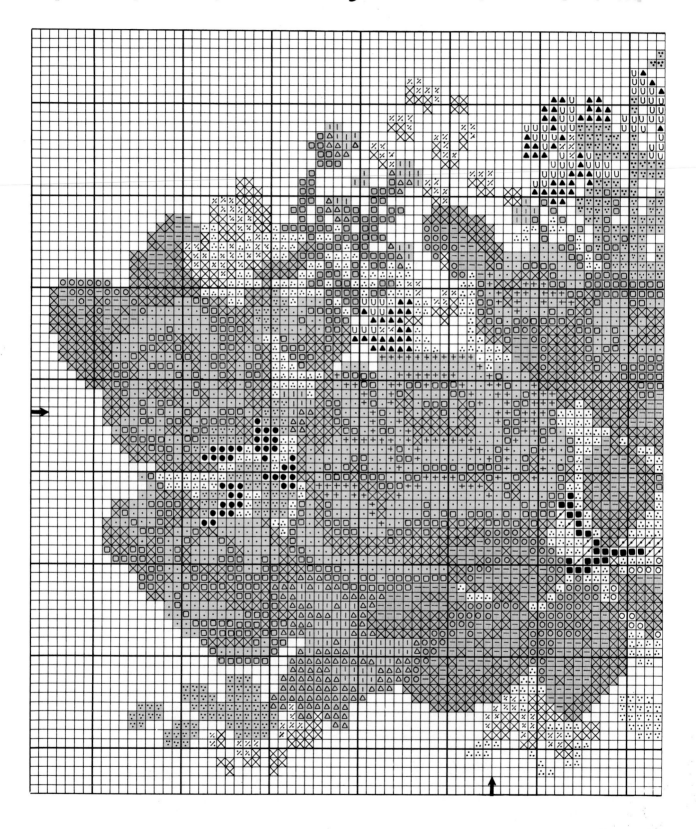

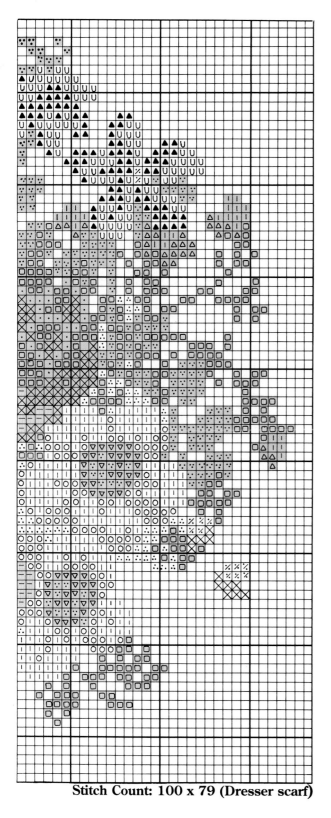

Stitch Count: 100 x 79 (Dresser scarf)

Mirror

Stitched on driftwood Belfast Linen 32 over two threads, the finished design size is 4¼" x 4⅛". The fabric was cut 12" x 17". More than one thread represented by a single symbol on the code and graph indicates blending; note the number of strands used.

Materials
(for one mirror)

Completed design on driftwood Belfast Linen 32; matching thread
12" x 17" piece of unstitched driftwood Belfast Linen 32
Wooden hand mirror frame (see Suppliers)
⅜ yard of fleece
5¾"-wide mirror
1¾ yards of pink braid
Hot glue gun and glue
Tracing paper
Dressmaker's pen

Vanity Set

Directions

1. Trace hand mirror frame outline to make pattern; cut out . Place pattern over design piece, centering design in mirror head. Trace pattern onto design piece. Adding 1" to all edges, cut out mirror back. Repeat on unstitched linen for mirror front. From fleece, cut two frame pieces and two mirror head pieces. Trim ⅛" from one fleece head and ¼" from the other.

2. To cover mirror back, glue one fleece frame piece to mirror frame. Center and glue smaller fleece head, then larger one, to mirror back. Lay design piece (right side down) on a flat surface. Place mirror frame (fleece side down) on wrong side of design piece. Wrap fabric around edges to frame front and glue in place, smoothing fabric.

3. To cover mirror front, press seam allowance over on unstitched linen front piece, clipping curves as needed. Insert remaining fleece under pressed seam allowance. Place linen/fleece (fleece side down) on frame front and slipstitch pressed (folded) edges to design piece edges. Center and glue mirror glass to mirror head front.

4. Measure around covered frame edge. Cut a length of braid to fit. Slipstitch braid over seam line joining mirror front to design piece. Repeat for mirror glass, gluing braid around mirror glass edge. With remaining braid, glue a length to mirror back across head where handle joins; see photo.

Anchor		DMC (used for sample)	
		Step 1: Cross-stitch (2 strands)	
933	U	3774	Peach Pecan-med.
337	▲	3778	Terra Cotta
892	I	225	Shell Pink-vy. lt.
893	+	224	Shell Pink-lt.
893 / 894	□	224 / 223	Shell Pink-lt. (1 strand)+ Shell Pink-med. (1 strand)
894	✕	223	Shell Pink-med.
968	O	778	Antique Mauve-vy. lt.
870	▽	3042	Antique Violet-lt.
871	∴	3041	Antique Violet-med.
842	□	3013	Khaki Green-lt.
875	∴	503	Blue Green-med.
876	●	502	Blue Green
858	–	524	Fern Green-vy. lt.
859 / 862	✕	522 / 520	Fern Green (1 strand)+ Fern Green-dk. (1 strand)
892 / 885	·	225 / 739	Shell Pink-vy. lt. (1 strand)+ Tan-ultra vy. lt. (1 strand)
885	⁒	739	Tan-ultra vy. lt.
942	✕	738	Tan-vy. lt.

Vanity Set

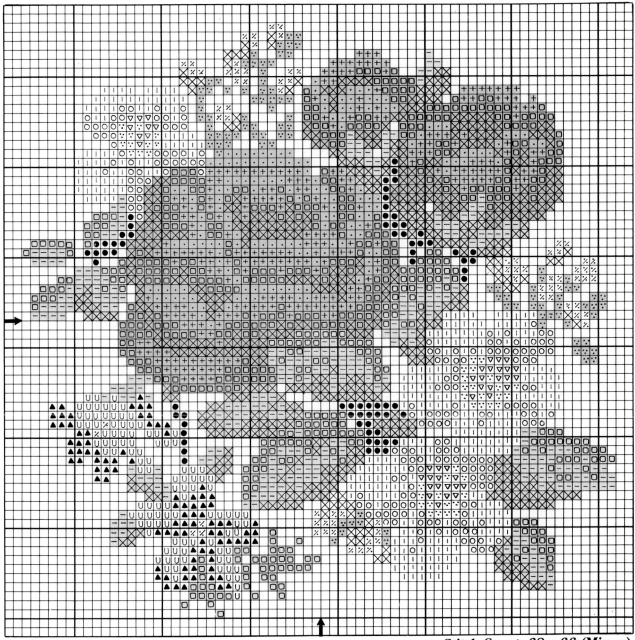

Stitch Count: 68 x 66 (Mirror)

Country Pinafore

Stitched on Wedgwood Murano 30 over two threads, the finished design size is 2⅛" x 1⅞" for each motif. The fabric was cut 22" x 12". Stitch motifs 2½" from one 22" edge and ⅜" apart across fabric width.

Materials

Completed design on Wedgwood Murano 30; matching thread
¼ yard of unstitched Wedgwood Murano 30
1¾ yards of ³⁄₁₆"-wide delft blue satin ribbon
¾ yard of 1"-wide purple French ribbon
1"-wide wood heart cutout
Acrylic paints
Sponges
4"-wide straw hat
Assorted dried fruits and flowers
Hot glue gun and glue
Tracing paper
Dressmaker's pen
6"-wide wire doll hanger

Directions
All seams are ¼".

1. Trim design to 20½" x 10½" with lower edge of design 1" from 20½" edge. Trace patterns. From unstitched Murano, cut two bodice ruffles, two bodices and a 32" x 2½" strip for skirt ruffle. Cut blue ribbon into one 12" and three 15" lengths. Cut purple ribbon into one 7" and one 20" length.

2. For skirt, stitch design piece with right sides facing and short raw edges aligned. (This seam is the center back; the long edge opposite the design will be the waist.) Mark center front of skirt at waist. Sew gathering threads on waist and gather to 11".

3. Join skirt ruffle piece end-to-end. Stitch gathering threads on one edge, gathering to fit skirt bottom. Stitch ruffle to skirt bottom with right sides facing and raw edges aligned. Fold ⅛" double to wrong side on remaining ruffle edge; hem.

4. For bodice ruffles, fold ⅛" double to wrong side of curved edge of each ruffle; hem. Sew gathering threads on straight edge of each ruffle and gather to 4".

5. Sandwich each ruffle between bodice pieces, with raw edges aligned and ruffle ends 2" from bodice ends. Stitch, catching ruffle in seam. Repeat for remaining ruffle. Stitch inside long raw edges of bodice pieces. Clip corners. Turn. Topstitch all edges. Mark center front of bodice at waist.

6. With right sides facing, align center back skirt seam between bodice backs, matching center front marks. Stitch.

7. Beginning and ending at center back, slipstitch each edge of 12" blue ribbon length over waist seam. Tie three bows from 15" lengths. Tack one at center back seam and one at each outside bodice front edge; see photo.

8. Sponge paint the heart cutout as desired. Allow to dry. Center and hot glue to bodice front.

9. For hat, fold the 7" length of purple ribbon in half horizontally; glue around crown for band. Tie a bow with 20" length; trim ends. Glue to band. Glue fruits or flowers to bow. Hang the pinafore with hat tacked to it.

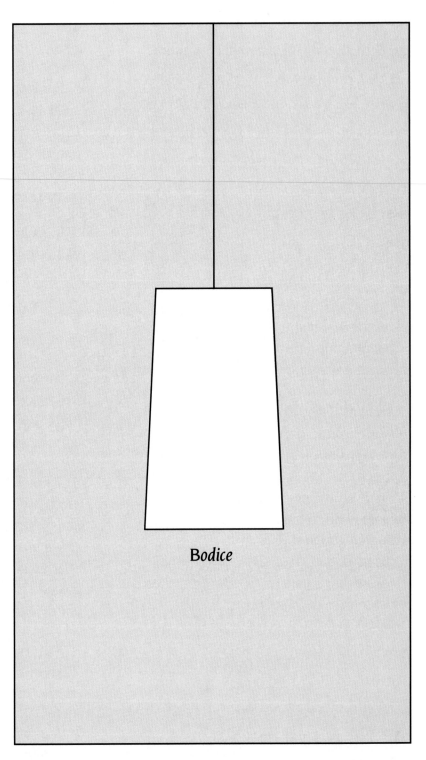

Bodice

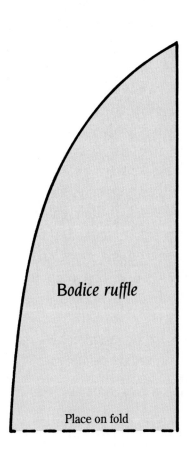

Bodice ruffle

Place on fold

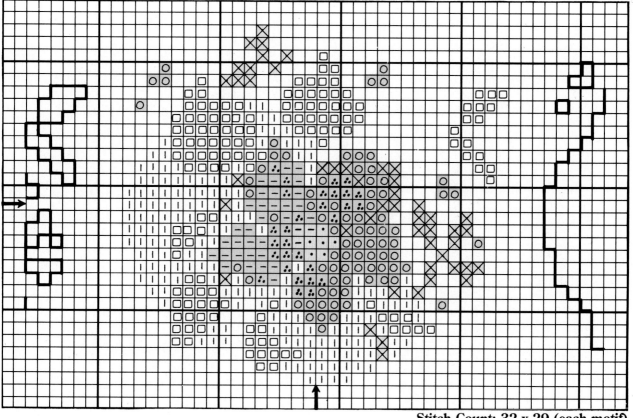

Stitch Count: 32 x 29 (each motif)

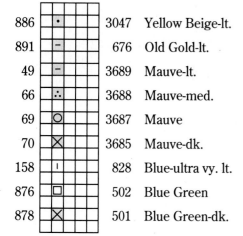

Anchor		DMC (used for sample)	
		Step 1: Cross-stitch (2 strands)	
886	•	3047	Yellow Beige-lt.
891	−	676	Old Gold-lt.
49	−	3689	Mauve-lt.
66	∴	3688	Mauve-med.
69	O	3687	Mauve
70	X	3685	Mauve-dk.
158	I	828	Blue-ultra vy. lt.
876	□	502	Blue Green
878	X	501	Blue Green-dk.

Dolled Up Quilt

Stitched on Waste Canvas 14 on tan fabric, the finished design size is 4⅞" x 6⅝" for each motif. The fabric was cut 11" x 11" for each. Cut nine. See Step 1 of Directions before stitching.

Materials

Eight completed designs on tan fabric
2 yards of melon fabric; matching thread
⅝ yard of tan fabric; matching thread
⅛ yard of green fabric
¼ yard of lavender fabric
1 yard of fleece
Embroidery floss
Assorted lace, trim, buttons
Fabric permanent pens
Dressmaker's pen
Cardboard

Directions
All seams are ¼".

1. Using one of each DMC color, stitch a motif in each of eight squares. Sign ninth square. Embellish each doll as desired.
    DMC used for sample(2 strands):
      758 Terra Cotta-lt.
    3688 Mauve-med.
     210 Lavender-med.
     799 Delft-med.
     959 Seagreen-med.
     989 Forest Green
     435 Brown-vy. lt.
     840 Beige Brown-med.

2. Make templates. Cut the following fabrics:
Melon: 36" square for back, eight 3" x 9" pieces, thirty-two 3" x 3½" pieces, 1¾"-wide bias for 4¼ yards of binding
Tan: Eight 3" squares
Green: 24 of Template A
Lavender: 96 of Template B
Fleece: 36" square.

3. Make 24 lavender and green diamond blocks (**Diagram 1**). To 16 blocks, attach one 3" x 3½" melon piece to two opposite sides (**Diagram 2**). Set aside.

4. Trim each 11" x 11" block to 9" x 9", with design centered. Join three 9" tan design squares and two 3" x 9" melon sashing strips to make top row (**Diagram 3**). Repeat for bottom row. Join three 9" tan square blocks and two diamond/melon strips to make middle row (**Diagram 4**).

5. Join three diamond/melon strips, two diamond blocks and two 3" tan squares to make top border row (**Diagram 5**). Repeat for bottom border row.

6. Join one diamond/melon strip, two 3" x 9" melon strips, two 3" tan squares and two diamond blocks for sashing strip (**Diagram 6**). Repeat for second sashing strip.

7. Assemble quilt top in rows (**Diagram 7**). Layer quilt back (wrong side up), fleece and quilt top (right side up). Baste. Quilt in-the-ditch on all sashing and border seams, using matching thread.

8. Bind the quilt, mitering corners.

Dolled Up Quilt

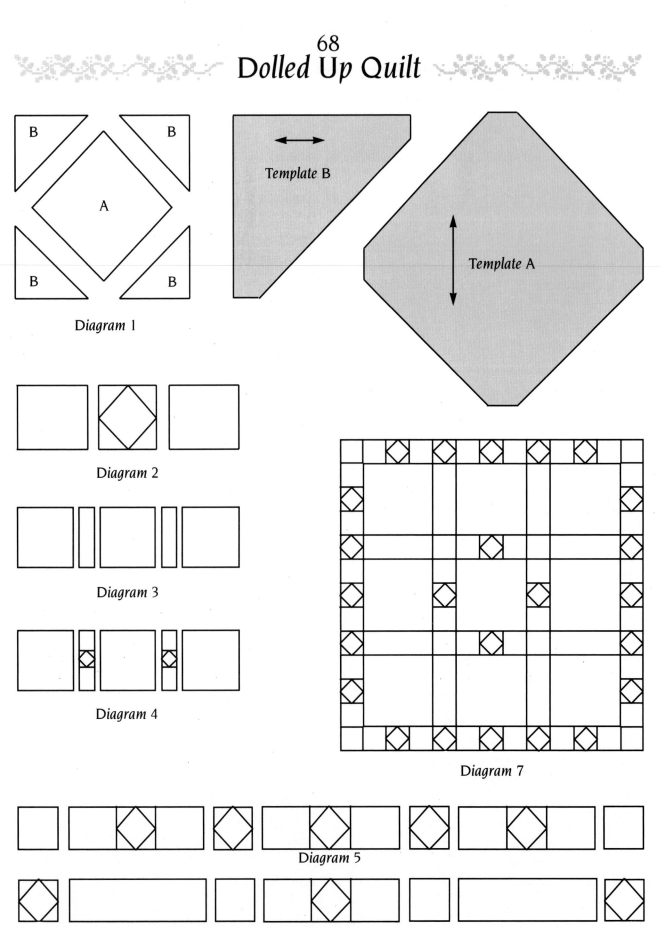

Diagram 1

Template B

Template A

Diagram 2

Diagram 3

Diagram 4

Diagram 7

Diagram 5

Diagram 6

Dolled Up Quilt

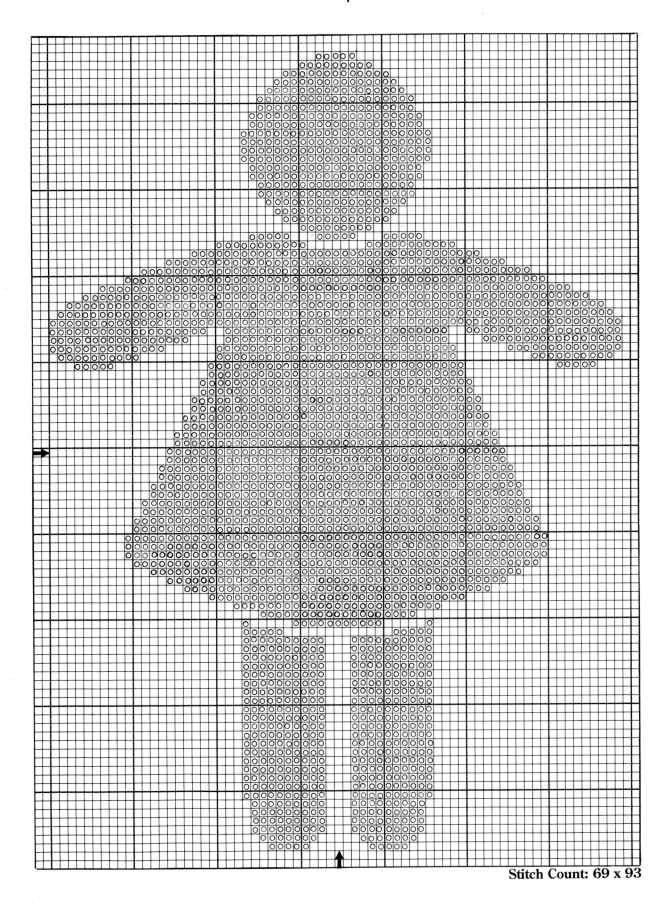

Stitch Count: 69 x 93

Spring Tablecloth

Stitched on Vanessa-Ann Damask 28 over two threads, the finished design size is 4¾" x 4¾" for each design. See **Diagram** for placement. The fabric was cut 58" x 58". (Width and length measurements each include five whole blocks.) The colored line surrounding designs on graph indicates fabric weave outline of each block. Center each design in each woven block. See Suppliers for fabric.

Materials

Completed designs on Vanessa-Ann Damask 28; matching thread
6¼ yards of 2¼"-wide cream scalloped bridal lace

Directions

1. Trim selvages from design piece and clean finish all raw edges.

2. Beginning at one corner, slipstitch scalloped pattern of lace to edge of afghan, pleating at each corner.

Diagram

S=Salmon   P=Pink
V=Violet   M=Mauve

Spring Tablecloth

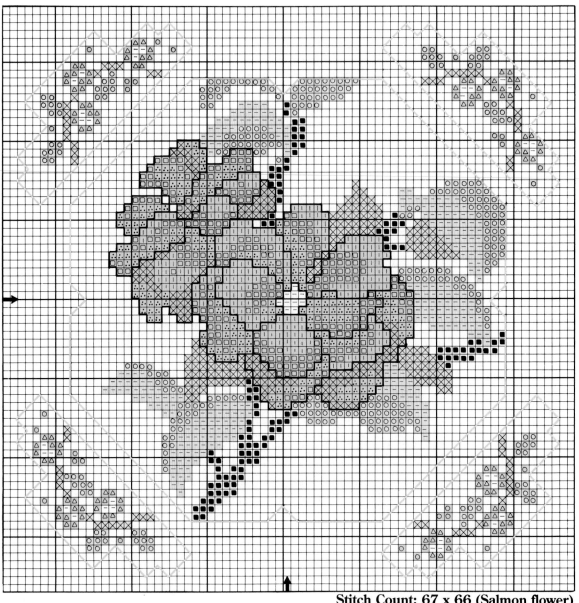

Stitch Count: 67 x 66 (Salmon flower)

Salmon Flower

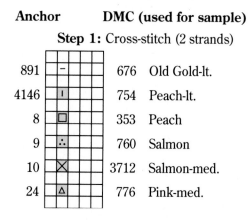

Anchor		DMC (used for sample)	
		Step 1: Cross-stitch (2 strands)	
891	–	676	Old Gold-lt.
4146	I	754	Peach-lt.
8	□	353	Peach
9	∴	760	Salmon
10	X	3712	Salmon-med.
24	△	776	Pink-med.

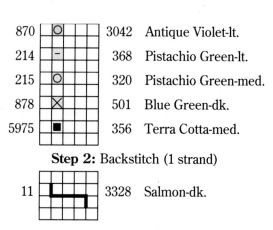

Anchor		DMC (used for sample)	
870	O	3042	Antique Violet-lt.
214	–	368	Pistachio Green-lt.
215	O	320	Pistachio Green-med.
878	X	501	Blue Green-dk.
5975	■	356	Terra Cotta-med.

Step 2: Backstitch (1 strand)

11	⌐	3328	Salmon-dk.

Spring Tablecloth

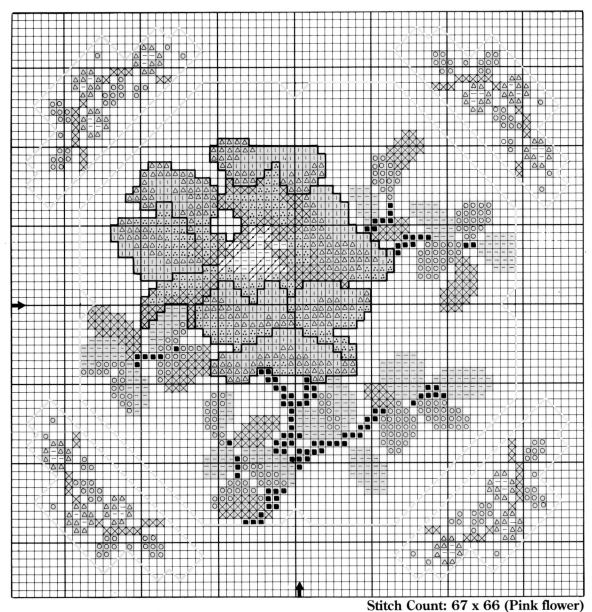

Stitch Count: 67 x 66 (Pink flower)

Pink Flower

Anchor **DMC (used for sample)**

Step 1: Cross-stitch (2 strands)

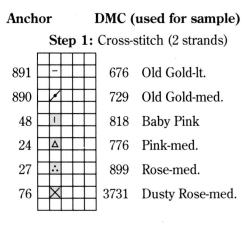

891	–	676	Old Gold-lt.
890	╱	729	Old Gold-med.
48	I	818	Baby Pink
24	△	776	Pink-med.
27	∴	899	Rose-med.
76	✕	3731	Dusty Rose-med.

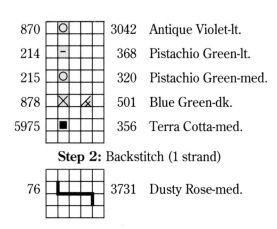

870	○	3042	Antique Violet-lt.
214	–	368	Pistachio Green-lt.
215	○	320	Pistachio Green-med.
878	✕ ╱	501	Blue Green-dk.
5975	■	356	Terra Cotta-med.

Step 2: Backstitch (1 strand)

| 76 | ⌐ | 3731 | Dusty Rose-med. |

Spring Tablecloth

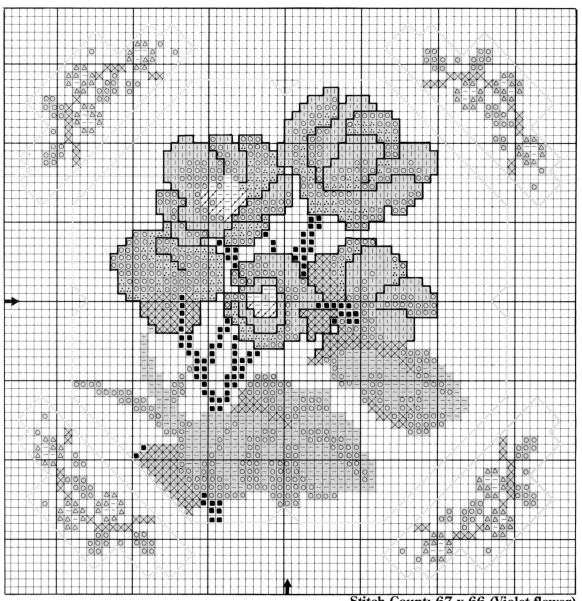

Stitch Count: 67 x 66 (Violet flower)

Violet Flower

Anchor		DMC (used for sample)
Step 1: Cross-stitch (2 strands)		
891	−	676 Old Gold-lt.
890	╱	729 Old Gold-med.
24	△	776 Pink-med.
869	I	3743 Antique Violet-vy. lt.
870	○	3042 Antique Violet-lt.
871	∴	3041 Antique Violet-med.

Anchor		DMC
872	⊠	3740 Antique Violet-dk.
214	−	368 Pistachio Green-lt.
215	○	320 Pistachio Green-med.
878	⊠	501 Blue Green-dk.
5975	■	356 Terra Cotta-med.

Step 2: Backstitch (1 strand)

872	⌐	3740 Antique Violet-dk.

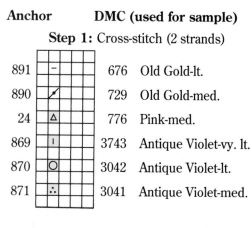
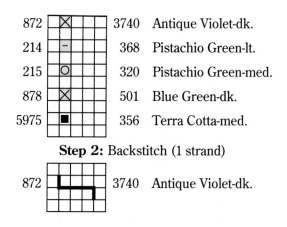

Spring Tablecloth

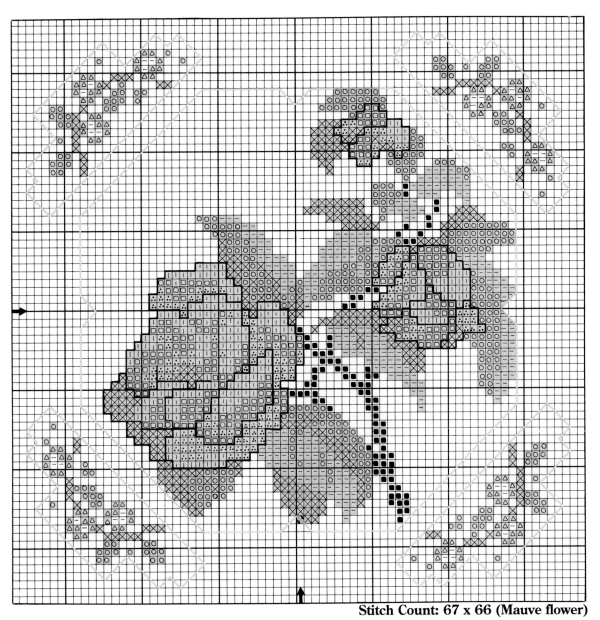

Stitch Count: 67 x 66 (Mauve flower)

Mauve Flower

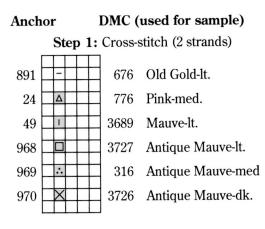

Anchor		DMC (used for sample)	
Step 1: Cross-stitch (2 strands)			
891	–	676	Old Gold-lt.
24	△	776	Pink-med.
49	I	3689	Mauve-lt.
968	□	3727	Antique Mauve-lt.
969	∴	316	Antique Mauve-med
970	X	3726	Antique Mauve-dk.

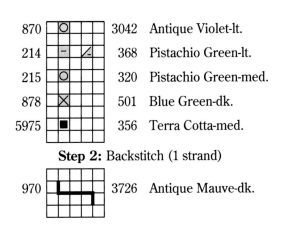

Anchor		DMC	
870	○	3042	Antique Violet-lt.
214	– /	368	Pistachio Green-lt.
215	○	320	Pistachio Green-med.
878	X	501	Blue Green-dk.
5975	■	356	Terra Cotta-med.
Step 2: Backstitch (1 strand)			
970	⌐	3726	Antique Mauve-dk.

Summer

The pace of life slows half a beat as we enjoy luxuriously long, summer days. This season embraces joyous occasions like weddings and anniversaries, the patriotic pride of the Fourth of July, and the warm and loving reassurance of Father's Day. Salute summer by picking from an array of projects that make wonderful gifts to give (or keep them all for yourself!). You'll find a delightful assortment of designs and colors too!

Summer Banner

Stitched on cream Country Aida 7, the finished design size is 13⅞" x 30⅝". The fabric was cut 20" x 45". See Suppliers for specialty thread and fabric.

Materials

Completed design on cream Country Aida 7; matching thread
2½ yards of coordinating fabric; matching thread
1¼ yards of fleece
1¼ yards of fusible interfacing
2⅜ yards of large cording
16½" length of 1¼"-wide wooden closet rod
Two 1½" x 4½" wooden finials
Glue
Acrylic paints
Paintbrushes

Directions

All seams are ¼".

1. Complete Steps 1-5 of Directions for Spring Banner on page 12.

Paternayan Persian Yarn
(used for sample)

Step 1: Cross-stitch (1 strand)

260	White
756	Old Gold-vy. lt.
703	Butterscotch-lt.
702	Butterscotch-med.
724	Autumn yellow
720	Autumn yellow-vy. dk.
812	Sunrise-med.
811	Sunrise-dk.
821	Tangerine-dk.
820	Tangerine- vy. dk.
843	Salmon
842	Salmon-med.
841	Salmon-dk.
332	Lavender
341	Periwinkle-dk.
652	Olive Green
650	Olive Green-vy.dk.
692	Loden Green
691	Loden Green-dk.
690	Loden Green-vy.dk.
883	Ginger
881	Ginger-vy.dk.
310	Black DMC Pearl Cotton #8 (4 strands)

Step 2: Backstitch (1 strand)

821	Tangerine-dk. (orange flowers)
652	Olive Green (white flowers)
310	Black DMC Pearl Cotton #8 (bee)

Step 3: French Knot (1 strand)

Summer Banner

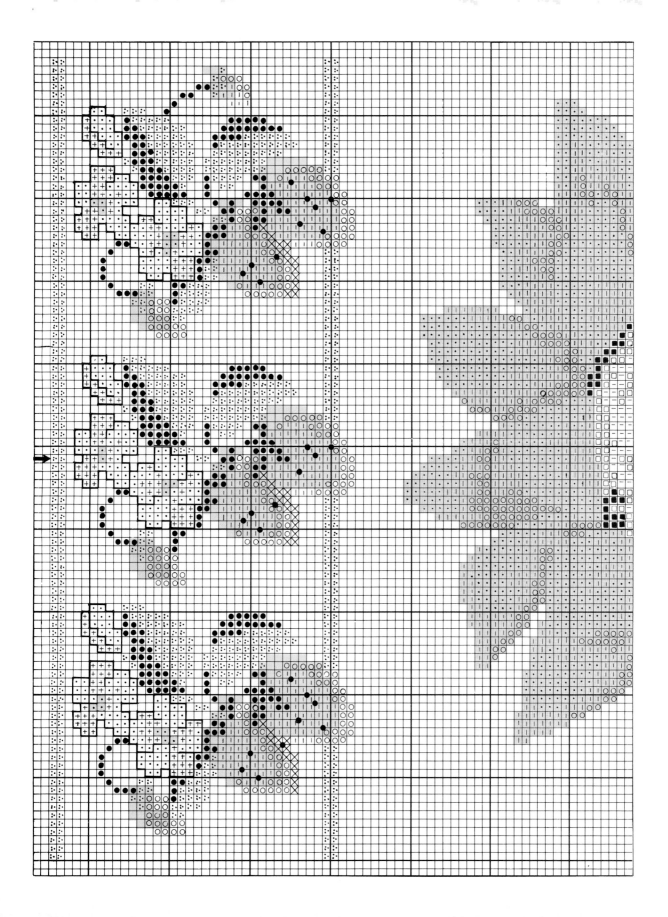

Summer Banner

Summer Banner

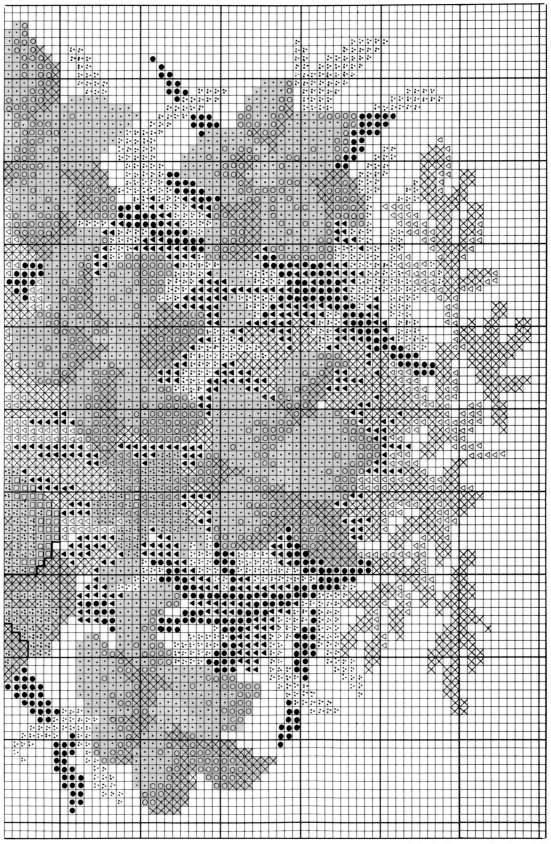

Stitch Count: 97 x 214

June Catnaps

Stitched on cream Murano 30 over two threads, the finished design size is 4⅝" x 6⅝". The fabric was cut 11" x 13". See March Charm on page 18 for cutout instructions.

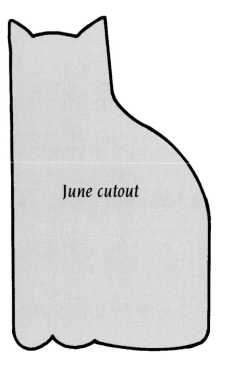

June cutout

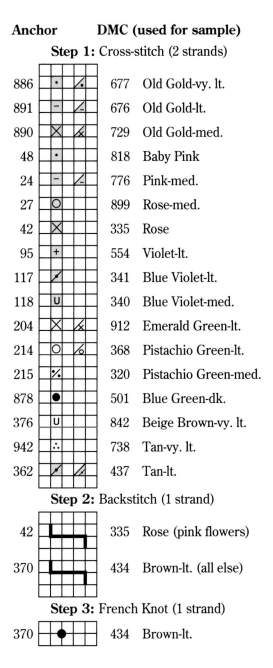

Anchor			DMC (used for sample)	
Step 1: Cross-stitch (2 strands)				
886	·	⁄	677	Old Gold-vy. lt.
891	–	⁄	676	Old Gold-lt.
890	X	⁄	729	Old Gold-med.
48	·		818	Baby Pink
24	–	⁄	776	Pink-med.
27	O		899	Rose-med.
42	X		335	Rose
95	+		554	Violet-lt.
117	⁄		341	Blue Violet-lt.
118	U		340	Blue Violet-med.
204	X	⁄	912	Emerald Green-lt.
214	O	⁄	368	Pistachio Green-lt.
215	⁒		320	Pistachio Green-med.
878	●		501	Blue Green-dk.
376	U		842	Beige Brown-vy. lt.
942	∴		738	Tan-vy. lt.
362	⁄	⁄	437	Tan-lt.
Step 2: Backstitch (1 strand)				
42			335	Rose (pink flowers)
370			434	Brown-lt. (all else)
Step 3: French Knot (1 strand)				
370	●		434	Brown-lt.

June Catnaps

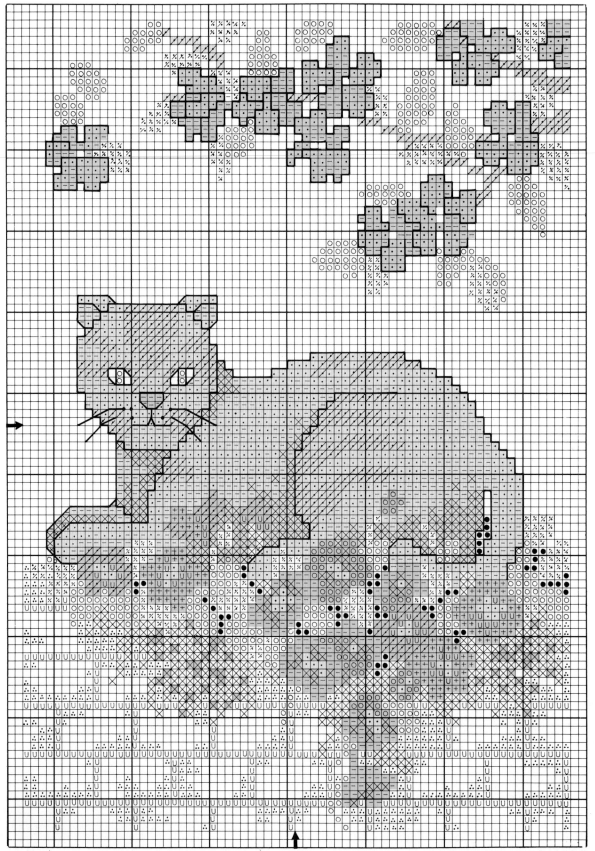

Stitch Count: 70 x 100

Daddy's Girl

Daddy's Girl

Stitched on celery Linda 27 over two threads, the finished design size is 8⅝" x 7¾". The fabric was cut 15" x 14".

Materials

Completed design on celery Linda 27; matching thread
Wooden box (see Suppliers)
Acrylic paints
Paintbrushes
11½" x 8½" piece of fleece
11½" x 8½" piece of foam core
Glue
Staple gun

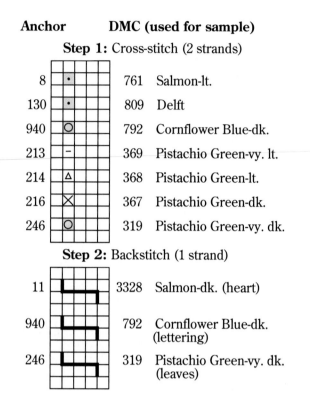

Anchor		DMC (used for sample)	
Step 1: Cross-stitch (2 strands)			
8	·	761	Salmon-lt.
130	·	809	Delft
940	O	792	Cornflower Blue-dk.
213	−	369	Pistachio Green-vy. lt.
214	△	368	Pistachio Green-lt.
216	X	367	Pistachio Green-dk.
246	O	319	Pistachio Green-vy. dk.
Step 2: Backstitch (1 strand)			
11		3328	Salmon-dk. (heart)
940		792	Cornflower Blue-dk. (lettering)
246		319	Pistachio Green-vy. dk. (leaves)

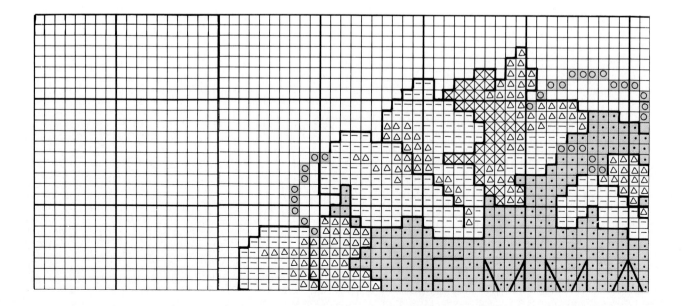

Daddy's Girl

Directions

1. Paint box with acrylic paints as desired.
Allow to dry.

2. To complete model, glue fleece to foam
core insert. Zigzag outer edges of design
piece, center and staple over insert,
following manufacturer's instructions.

Alphabet

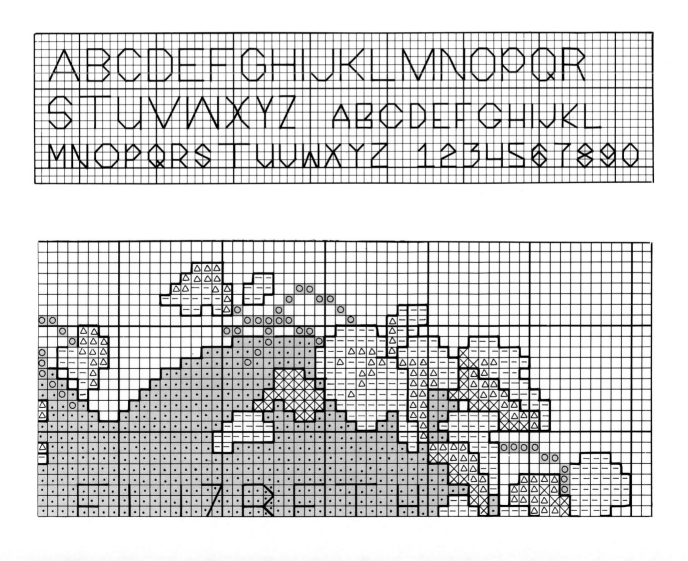

Daddy's Girl

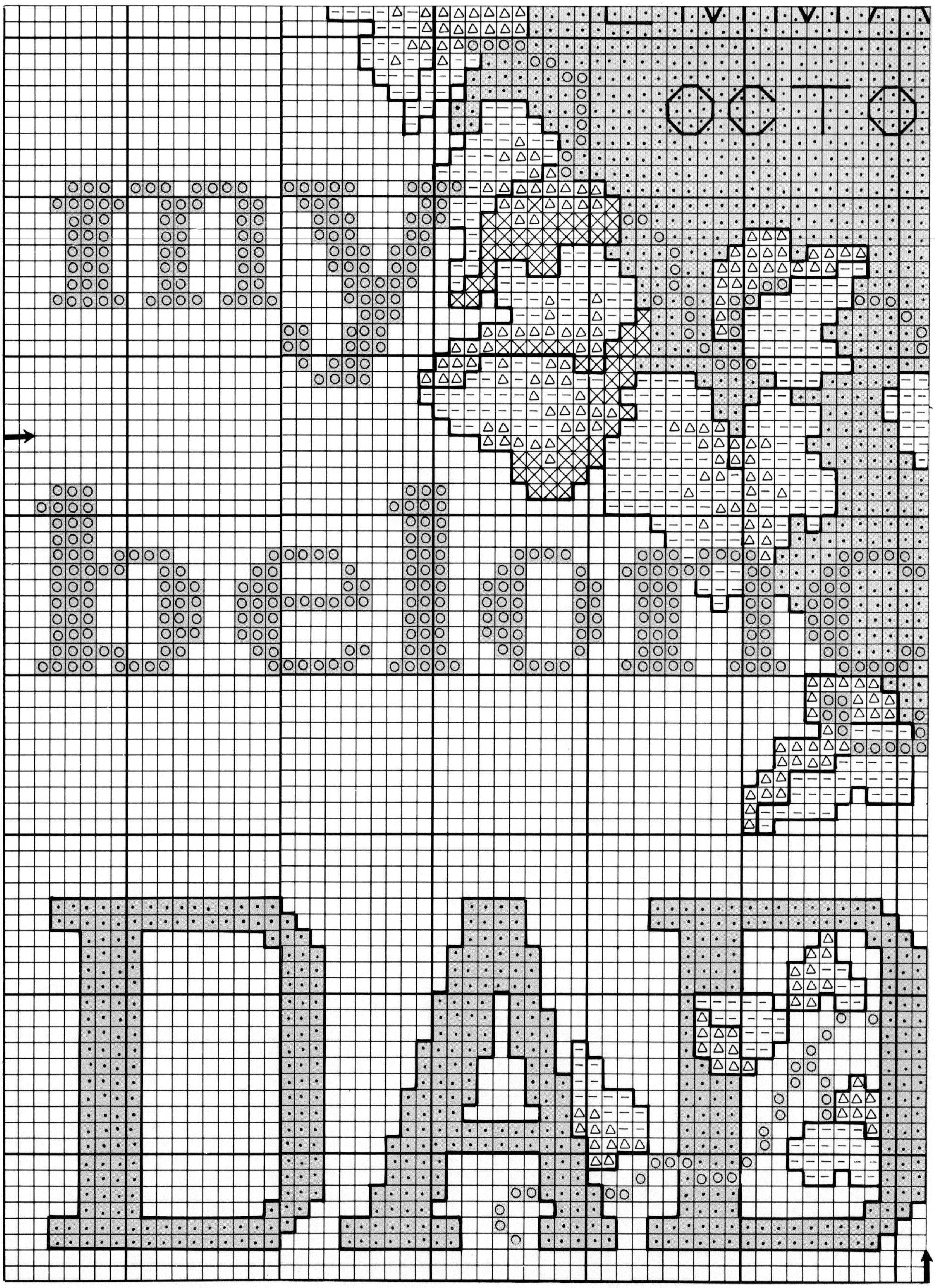

Daddy's Girl

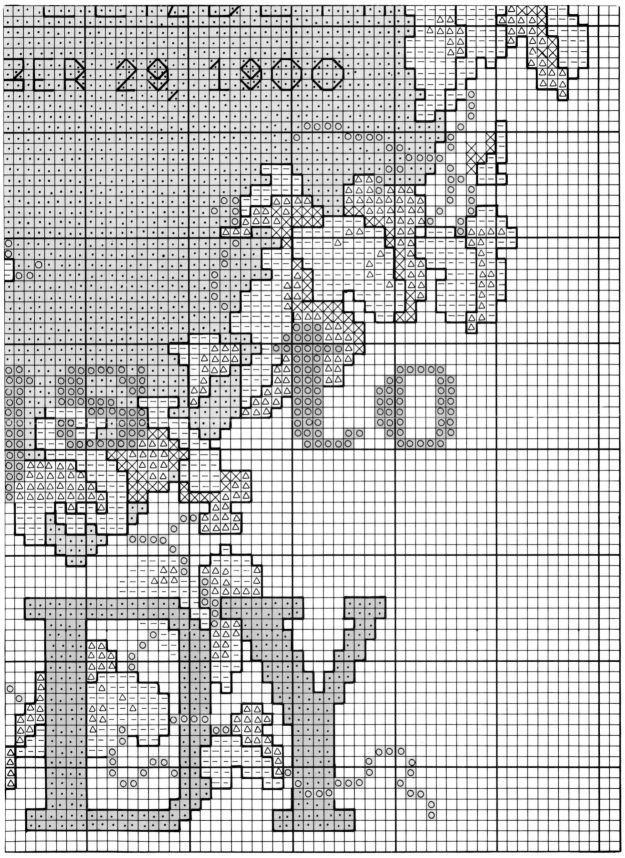

Stitch Count: 116 x 104

Summer
Flower
Set

Large Floral

Stitched on cream Murano 30 over two threads, the finished design size is 13⅛" x 10½". The fabric was cut 20" x 17". More than one thread represented by a single symbol on the code and graph indicates blending; note number of strands used.

Red Floral

Stitched on cream Murano 30 over two threads, the finished design size is 5⅜" x 7½". The fabric was cut 12" x 14". More than one thread represented by a single symbol on the code and graph indicates blending; note number of strands used.

Yellow Floral

Stitched on cream Murano 30 over two threads, the finished design size is 5⅜" x 7½". The fabric was cut 12" x 14". More than one thread represented by a single symbol on the code and graph indicates blending; note number of strands used.

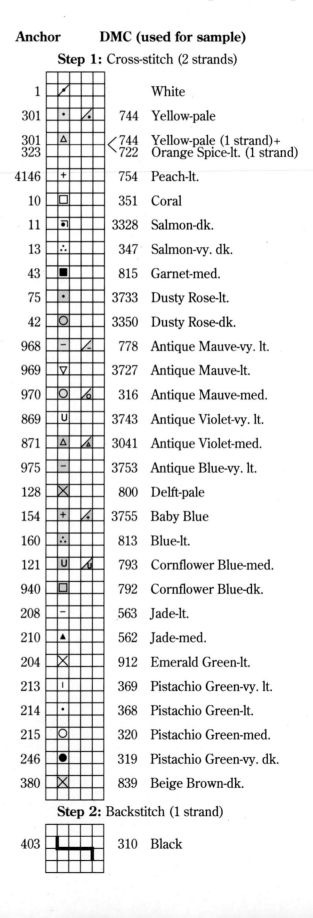

Anchor			DMC (used for sample)	

Step 1: Cross-stitch (2 strands)

Anchor			DMC	
1				White
301			744	Yellow-pale
301 301 323			⟨744 722	Yellow-pale (1 strand)+ Orange Spice-lt. (1 strand)
4146			754	Peach-lt.
10			351	Coral
11			3328	Salmon-dk.
13			347	Salmon-vy. dk.
43			815	Garnet-med.
75			3733	Dusty Rose-lt.
42			3350	Dusty Rose-dk.
968			778	Antique Mauve-vy. lt.
969			3727	Antique Mauve-lt.
970			316	Antique Mauve-med.
869			3743	Antique Violet-vy. lt.
871			3041	Antique Violet-med.
975			3753	Antique Blue-vy. lt.
128			800	Delft-pale
154			3755	Baby Blue
160			813	Blue-lt.
121			793	Cornflower Blue-med.
940			792	Cornflower Blue-dk.
208			563	Jade-lt.
210			562	Jade-med.
204			912	Emerald Green-lt.
213			369	Pistachio Green-vy. lt.
214			368	Pistachio Green-lt.
215			320	Pistachio Green-med.
246			319	Pistachio Green-vy. dk.
380			839	Beige Brown-dk.

Step 2: Backstitch (1 strand)

Anchor			DMC	
403			310	Black

Summer Flower Set

Large floral (top left)

Summer Flower Set

Large floral (top center)

Summer Flower Set

Large floral (top right)

Summer Flower Set

Large floral (bottom left)

Summer Flower Set

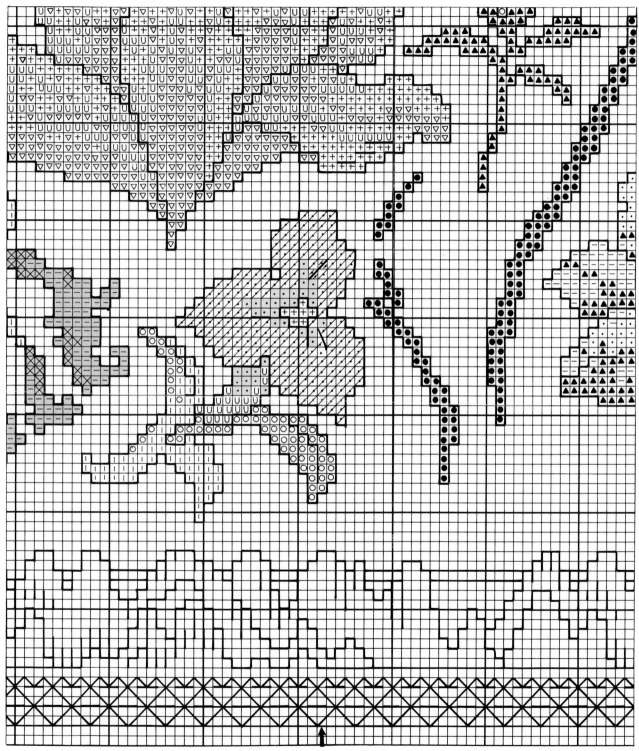

Large floral (bottom center)

Summer Flower Set

Large floral (bottom right)   **Stitch Count: 197 x 158**

Summer Flower Set

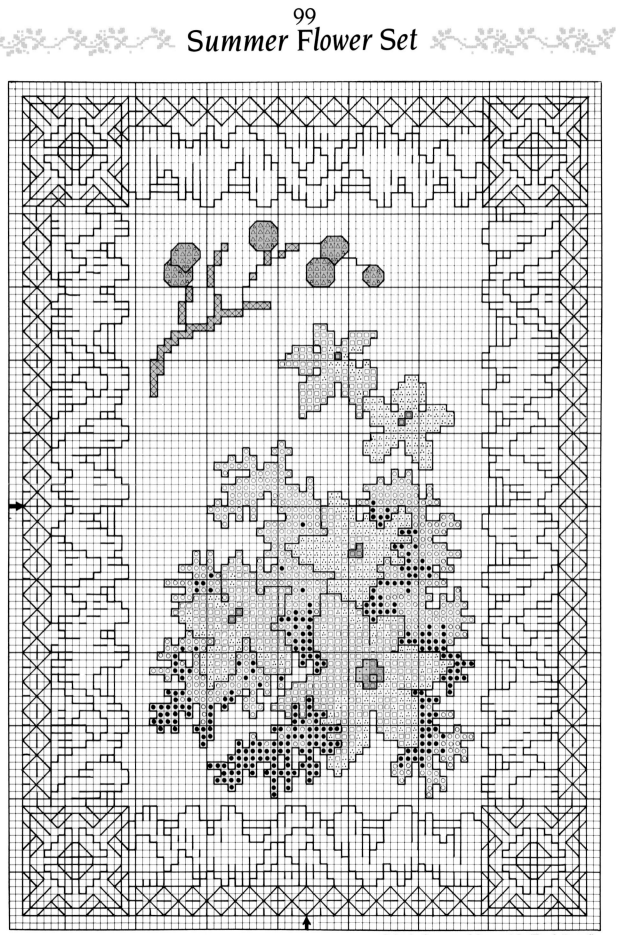

Stitch Count: 80 x 112 (Red floral)

Summer Flower Set

Stitch Count: 80 x 112 (Yellow floral)

Wedding Ensemble

Wedding Ensemble

Frame

Materials

Stitched on daffodil Damask Aida 18, the finished design size is 6⅝" x 6⅝". The fabric was cut 13" x 13".

Completed design on daffodil Damask Aida 18
Professionally cut mat; see Step 1 of Directions
Double-sided tape
Masking tape
Dressmaker's pen

Directions

1. Have a professional framer cut mat board. Outside edges should measure 8" square, with a 4¾"-wide circle centered for window.

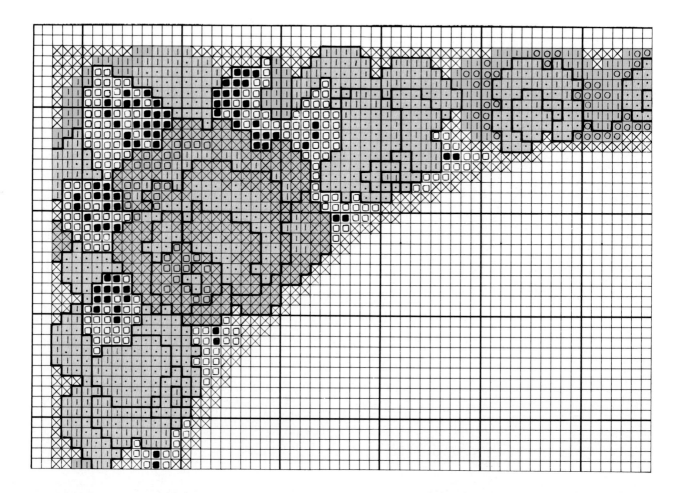

2. Trim design piece to 9½" square. Center mat on wrong side of design piece on flat surface and trace window edge. Then draw a smaller window 1" inside the first window. Cut on smaller circle pen line. Clip the fabric between the two circle pen lines at ⅜" intervals.

3. On wrong side of mat, place small strips of double-sided tape around window and outside edge of mat. Center right side of mat over wrong side of design. Fold design piece over all mat edges, pulling taut. Secure with masking tape. Place mat in ready-made frame or have professional framer complete.

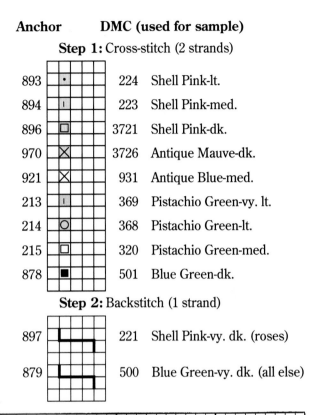

Anchor		DMC (used for sample)	
Step 1: Cross-stitch (2 strands)			
893	·	224	Shell Pink-lt.
894	I	223	Shell Pink-med.
896	□	3721	Shell Pink-dk.
970	⊠	3726	Antique Mauve-dk.
921	✕	931	Antique Blue-med.
213	I	369	Pistachio Green-vy. lt.
214	○	368	Pistachio Green-lt.
215	□	320	Pistachio Green-med.
878	■	501	Blue Green-dk.
Step 2: Backstitch (1 strand)			
897		221	Shell Pink-vy. dk. (roses)
879		500	Blue Green-vy. dk. (all else)

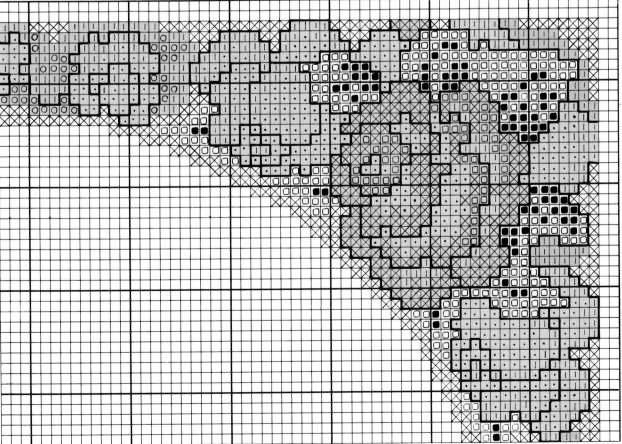

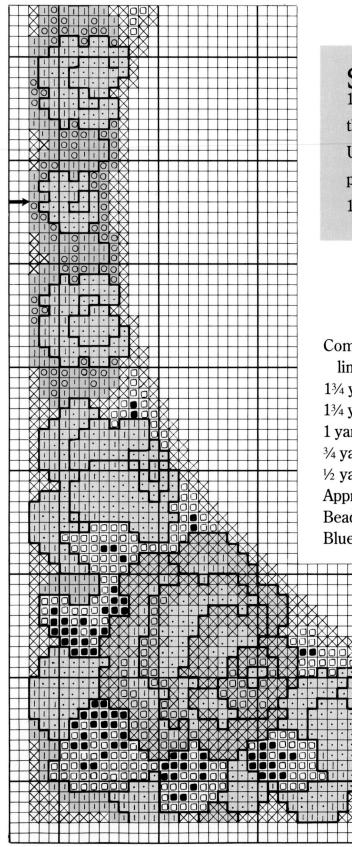

Handkerchief

Stitched on Waste Canvas 14 on a 12" x 12" cream linen handkerchief, the finished design size is 2" x 2". Using code on page103 and graph on page 109, stitch one rose on corner 1" from each edge.

Materials

Completed design on 12" x 12" cream
  linen handkerchief; matching thread
1¾ yards of 1½"-wide flat cream lace
1¾ yards of ⅛"-wide green silk ribbon
1 yard of ⅛"-wide burgundy silk ribbon
¾ yard of ⅛"-wide dusty rose silk ribbon
½ yard of ⅛"-wide cream silk ribbon
Approximately 100 blue glass seed beads
Beading needle
Blue thread

Wedding Ensemble

Directions

1. To attach lace and beads to handkerchief, see Step 2 of Directions for Ring Pillow on page 106.

2. Cut a 48" length of green ribbon. Slipstitch to handkerchief ¼" from outer edge.

3. Make one dusty rose and three burgundy spider web roses on motif. With cream thread, make a five-sided spoke (**Diagram 1**). Beginning at center, weave ribbon over and under to loosely fill spokes (**Diagram 2**).

4. For buds, make seven cream and nine dusty rose french knots from remaining ribbon, placing as desired. For leaves, lazy daisy stitch with remaining green ribbon around flowers; see photo.

Diagram 1　　　　**Diagram 2**

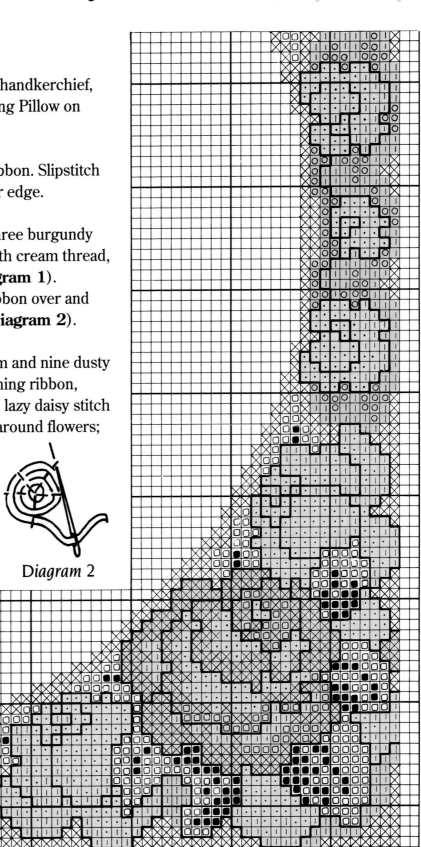

Stitch Count: 120 x 120 (Frame)

Ring Pillow

Stitched on daffodil Damask Aida 14, the finished design size is 8⅝" x 8⅝". The fabric was cut 15" x 15".

Materials

Completed design on daffodil Damask
  Aida 14; matching thread
9⅛"square of unstitched daffodil Damask
  Aida 14
1¼ yards of 1½"-wide flat cream lace
4 yards of ⅛"-wide cream satin ribbon

4 yards of 1⁄16 "-wide cream satin ribbon
Approximately 130 blue glass seed beads
Polyester stuffing
Beading needle
Blue thread

Directions

All seams are ¼".

1. Trim design piece to 9⅛" square with design centered. Stitch design piece to unstitched piece of daffodil Damask Aida 14 with right sides facing, leaving an opening. Clip corners. Turn. Stuff moderately. Slipstitch opening closed.

2. Slipstitch straight edge of lace to pillow seam, pleating at each corner. Add beads in groups of three, following design in lace.

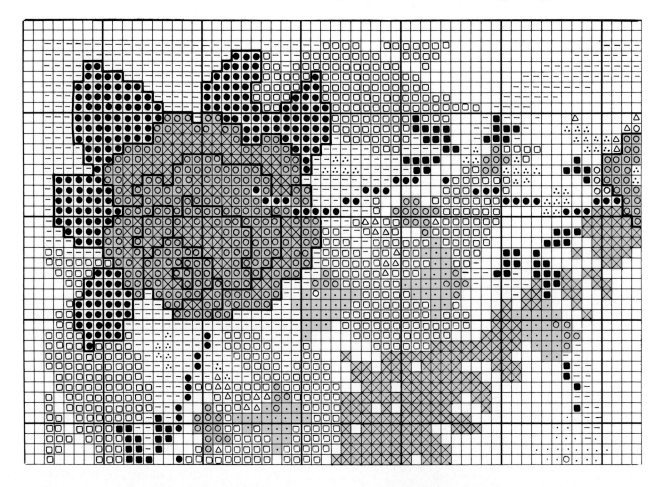

Wedding Ensemble

3. To make ring ties, cut two 18" pieces of ¹⁄₁₆ "-wide ribbon to each pillow corner. Tie a knot in center and 1" from each end of each ribbon. Tack each center knot 1½" apart in center of design.

4. To make each corner bow set, cut four 1 yard lengths of ⅛"-wide ribbon and four 24" lengths of ¹⁄₁₆ "-wide ribbon. Tie each 1 yard length into a small bow. Tie a knot in center of each 24" length. Tack one of each ribbon length to each pillow corner. Knot tails randomly.

Anchor		DMC (used for sample)	

Step 1: Cross-stitch (2 strands)

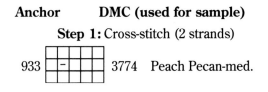

933	−	3774	Peach Pecan-med.

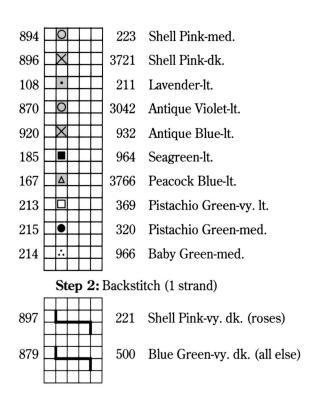

894	○	223	Shell Pink-med.
896	✕	3721	Shell Pink-dk.
108	·	211	Lavender-lt.
870	○	3042	Antique Violet-lt.
920	✕	932	Antique Blue-lt.
185	■	964	Seagreen-lt.
167	△	3766	Peacock Blue-lt.
213	□	369	Pistachio Green-vy. lt.
215	●	320	Pistachio Green-med.
214	∴	966	Baby Green-med.

Step 2: Backstitch (1 strand)

897		221	Shell Pink-vy. dk. (roses)
879		500	Blue Green-vy. dk. (all else)

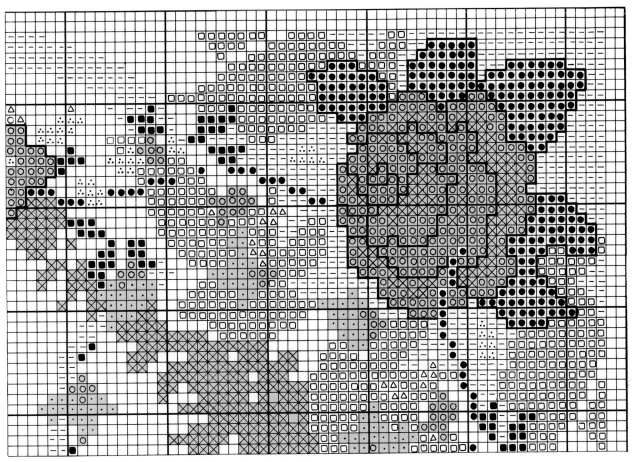

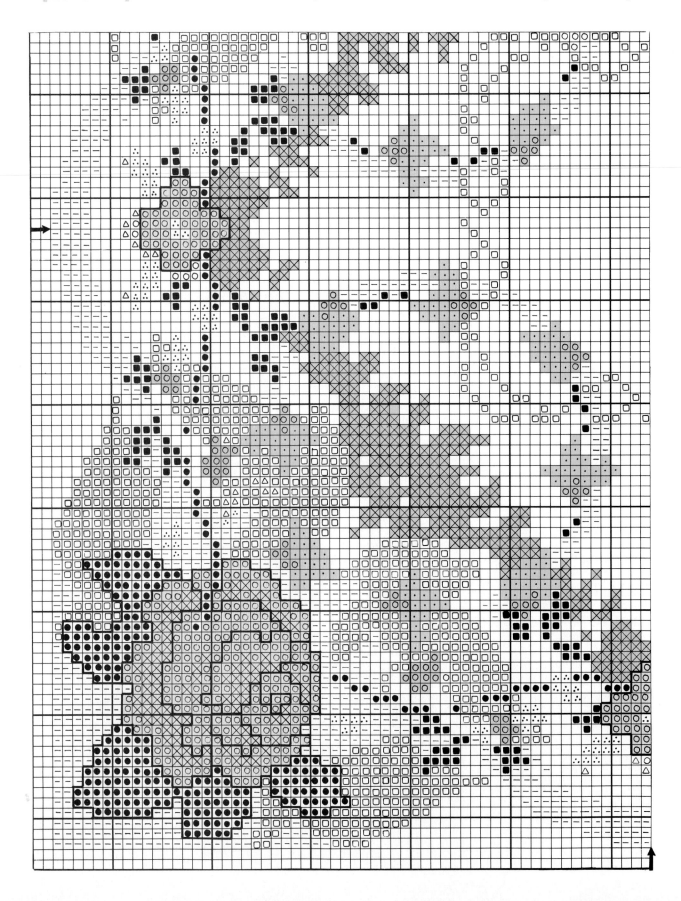

Wedding Ensemble

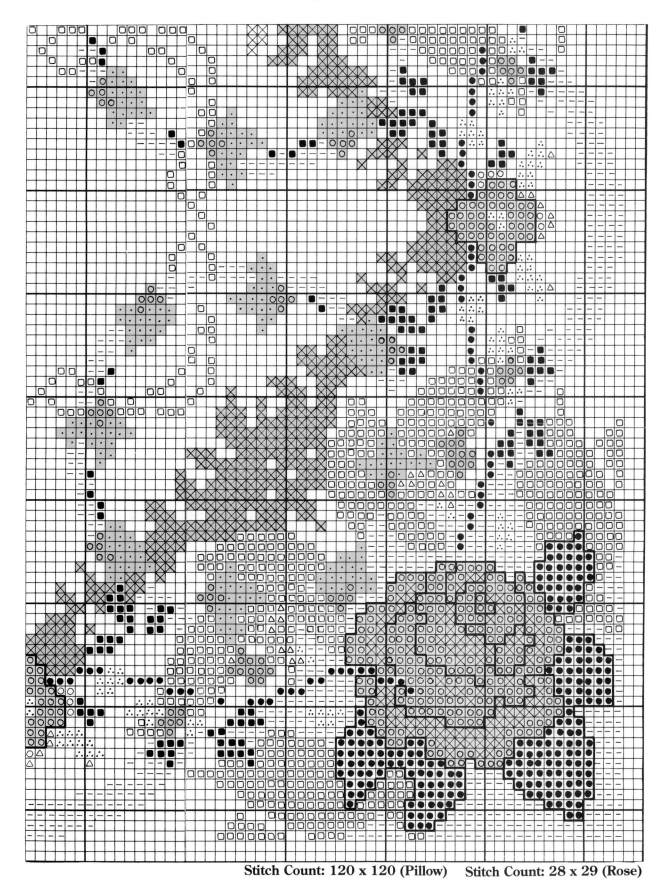

Stitch Count: 120 x 120 (Pillow)   **Stitch Count: 28 x 29 (Rose)**

Silver Anniversary

Stitched on cream Belfast Linen 32 over two threads, the finished design size is 11¼" x 6½". The fabric was cut 18" x 13". See Suppliers for specialty thread. More than one thread represented by a single symbol on code and graph indicates blending; note number of strands used. To complete, zigzag outer edges of design, center and glue as desired.

Anchor			DMC (used for sample)	

Step 1: Cross-stitch (2 strands)

887	+	⁄	3046 / 002HL	Yellow Beige-med. (1 strand)+ Metallic Gold Balger blending filament (1 strand)
933	c	⁄	3774	Peach Pecan-med.
4146	◆		950	Peach Pecan-dk.
324	⅔	⁄	922	Copper-lt.
339	□	⁄	920	Copper-med.
341	●		3777	Terra Cotta-vy. dk.
892	○	⁄	225	Shell Pink-vy. lt.
968	◇		<778 013	Antique Mauve-vy. lt.(1 strand)+ Metallic Beige Balger blending filament (1 strand)
896	△		3722	Shell Pink
897	✕		3721	Shell Pink-dk.
869	V		3743	Antique Violet-vy. lt.
871	••		3041	Antique Violet-med.
872	▼	⁄	3740	Antique Violet-dk.
101	▲		327	Antique Violet-vy. dk.
975	I	⁄	3753	Antique Blue-vy. lt.

921	•		931	Antique Blue-med.
922	◙	⁄	930	Antique Blue-dk.
928	■		598	Turquoise-lt.
779	⁄		926	Slate Green
875	U	⁄	503	Blue Green-med.
878	::		501	Blue Green-dk.
860	∴		<3053 043	Green Gray (1 strand)+ Metallic Confetti Green Balger blending filament (1 strand)
956	b	⁄	613	Drab Brown-lt.
882	•	⁄	407	Pecan
914	✕		3772	Pecan-med.
380	△	⁄	839	Beige Brown-dk.
397	-	⁄	3072	Beaver Gray-vy. lt.
399	•	⁄	318	Steel Gray-lt.
400	△		414	Steel Gray-dk.
401	✕	⁄	317	Pewter Gray

Step 2: Backstitch (1 strand)

236		3799	Pewter Gray-vy. dk.

Step 3: French Knot (1 strand)

236	●	3799	Pewter Gray-vy. dk.

Silver Anniversary

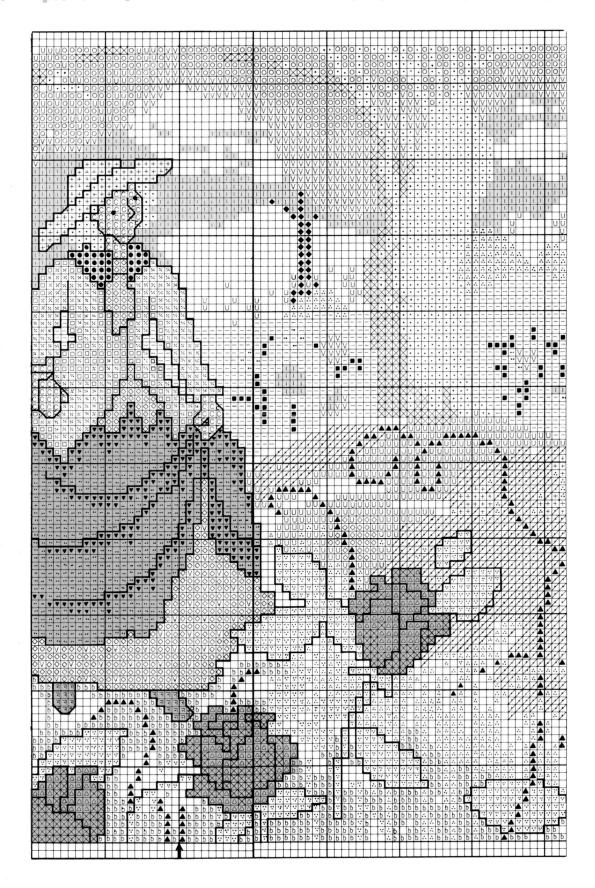

Silver Anniversary

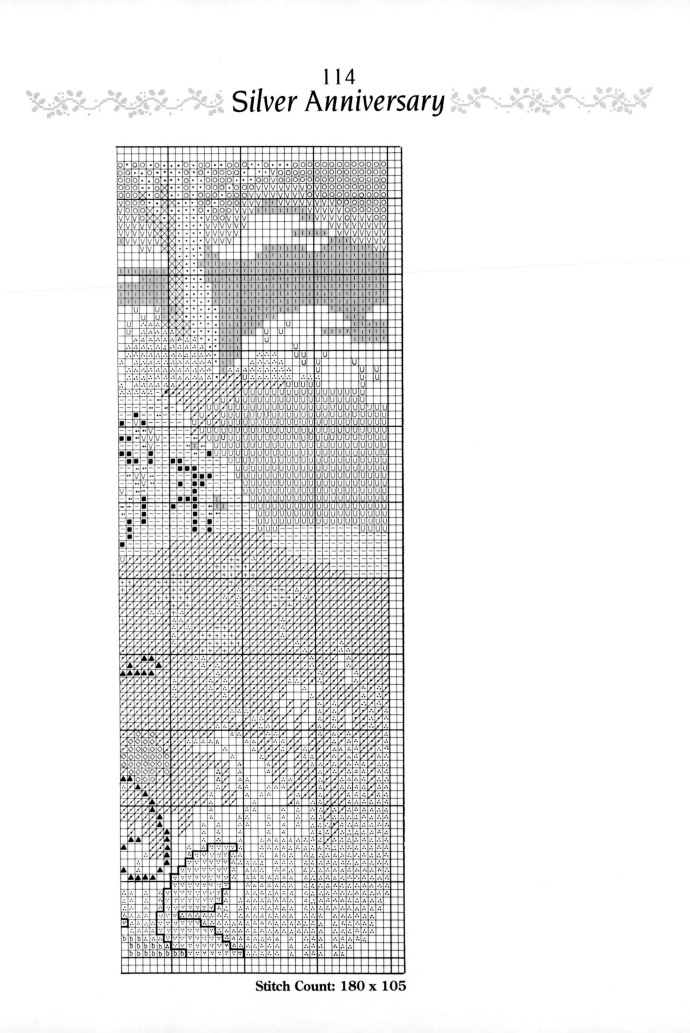

Stitch Count: 180 x 105

July Flagwaving

July Flagwaving

Stitched on cream Murano 30 over two threads, the finished design size is 4¾" x 6⅝". The fabric was cut 11" x 13". See March Charm on page 18 for cutout instructions.

July cutout

Anchor		DMC (used for sample)	
Step 1: Cross-stitch (2 strands)			
1	·		White
301	+	744	Yellow-pale
323	−	722	Orange Spice-lt.
42	✕	309	Rose-deep
47	○	304	Christmas Red-med.
158	△	747	Sky Blue-vy. lt.
159	□	3325	Baby Blue-lt.
921	✕	931	Antique Blue-med.
214	ı	966	Baby Green-med.
264	∴	772	Pine Green-lt.
843	╱	3364	Pine Green
246	●	986	Forest Green-vy. dk.
830	⁒	644	Beige Gray-med.
399	−	318	Steel Gray-lt.
400	○	317	Pewter Gray
Step 2: Backstitch (1 strand)			
401		413	Pewter Gray-dk.

117
July Flagwaving

Stitch Count: 71 x 100

Dresser Bow

Materials

Completed design on white Jobelan 28; matching thread
2½ yards of white taffeta
5" x 8" piece of fleece
Mat board
Dressmaker's pen
Hot glue gun and glue

Directions
All seams are ¼".

1. Trim design piece to 7½"-wide circle with design centered. Cut a 4¼"-wide and a 3½"-wide fleece circle. From mat board, cut a 4¼"-wide circle. Cut taffeta to 24" x 90".

2. To make design circle, center and glue larger fleece circle on mat board circle. Center and glue smaller fleece circle on larger circle. Stitch gathering threads around outer edges of design piece; zigzag edges. Center over fleece, pulling gathering thread and gluing to back of mat board circle. Set aside.

3. Fold taffeta in half with right sides facing and long raw edges aligned. Stitch on long edge to make a tube, leaving an opening in center back; do not turn. Position seam in center back and press (**Diagram 1**). Mark seam 5" from open end. Stitch a "V" (**Diagram 2**). Repeat on opposite end. Trim seams, clipping corners. Turn. Slipstitch opening closed. Press. Tie taffeta into a bow.

4. Tack circle to bow center. Attach bow to dresser; see photo.

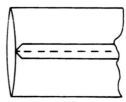

Diagram 1

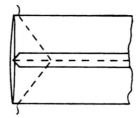

Diagram 2

Dresser Bow

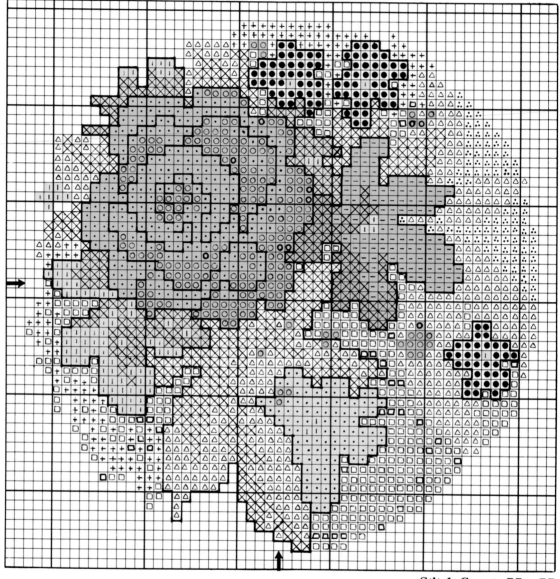

Stitch Count: 55 x 55

Anchor   **DMC (used for sample)**

Step 1: Cross-stitch (2 strands)

Anchor		DMC	
386	+	746	Off White
886	□	3047	Yellow Beige-lt.
4146	∴	754	Peach-lt.
968	•	778	Antique Mauve-vy. lt.
74	O	3354	Dusty Rose-vy. lt.
158	−	828	Blue-ultra vy. lt.
160	⊠	3761	Sky Blue-lt.
214	△	369	Pistachio Green-vy. lt.
203	☒	564	Jade-vy. lt.
213	I	504	Blue Green-lt.
875	✕	503	Blue Green-med.
942	●	738	Tan-vy. lt.
397	·	762	Pearl Gray-vy. lt.

Step 2: Backstitch (1 strand)

Anchor		DMC	
76		3731	Dusty Rose-med. (rose)
878		501	Blue Green-dk. (all else)

Patriotic Village

Large Building

Stitched on clear Plastic Canvas 7 over one mesh. The canvas was cut:

Roof (cut and stitch two) 6¾" x 2⅜"

Front (cut and stitch one) 5⅞" x 4½"

Back (cut and stitch one) 5⅞" x 4½"

Side (cut and stitch two) 2½" x 5⅝"

Ceiling (cut one) 5⅝" x 2½"

Bottom (cut one) 5⅝" x 2½"

Use five 7" x 7" pieces of plastic canvas for this building. Bold lines on graphs indicate cutting lines. See Suppliers for specialty thread and plastic canvas.

Materials

Six completed designs on clear Plastic
    Canvas 7; matching yarn
5⅝" x 2½" unstitched clear Plastic
    Canvas 7 (Ceiling)
5⅝" x 2½" unstitched clear Plastic
    Canvas 7 (Bottom)
Fine-tip marker
Hot glue gun and glue
Polyester stuffing

Directions

1. For each design piece, mark lightly on plastic canvas, following bold lines on graph. Cut carefully.

2. Overcast edges of all building pieces (see Step 2 of color code). Then whipstitch Front, Side, Back and Side together to form a shell. Whipstitch Ceiling to top edge. Whipstitch Roofs on one long edge and then to top of shell/Ceiling, forming an overhang. Glue as necessary. Stuff moderately. Whipstitch Bottom to bottom edge to complete building.

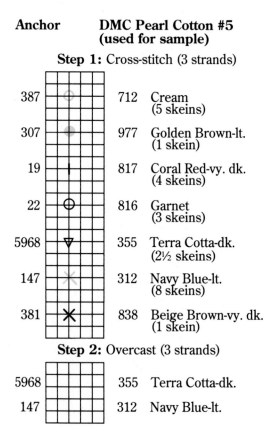

Anchor		DMC Pearl Cotton #5 (used for sample)	
Step 1: Cross-stitch (3 strands)			
387	◕	712	Cream (5 skeins)
307	◔	977	Golden Brown-lt. (1 skein)
19	|	817	Coral Red-vy. dk. (4 skeins)
22	⊕	816	Garnet (3 skeins)
5968	▽	355	Terra Cotta-dk. (2½ skeins)
147	✕	312	Navy Blue-lt. (8 skeins)
381	✖	838	Beige Brown-vy. dk. (1 skein)
Step 2: Overcast (3 strands)			
5968		355	Terra Cotta-dk.
147		312	Navy Blue-lt.

Patriotic Village

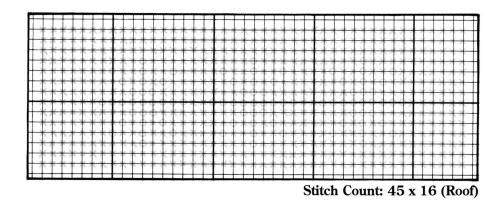

Stitch Count: 45 x 16 (Roof)

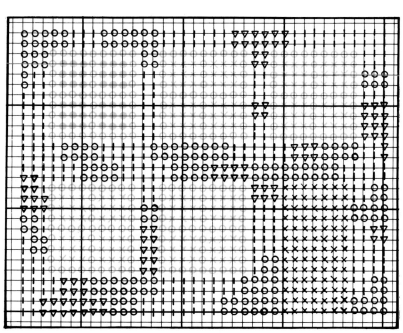

Stitch Count: 39 x 30 (Front and Back)

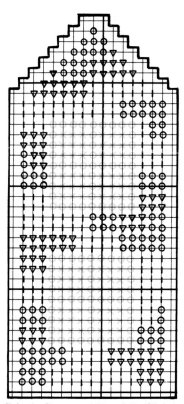

Stitch Count: 17 x 37 (Side)

Star Building

Stitched on clear Plastic Canvas 7 over one mesh. Use floss in parentheses for alternate building colors; see photo. The canvas was cut:

Front (cut and stitch one) 3⅜" x 2⅝"

Back (cut and stitch one) 3½" x 2⅝"

Side (cut and stitch two) 2¼" x 4"

Roof (cut and stitch two) 3½" x 1⅝"

Chimney Side (cut and stitch four)
   ½" x ⅞"

Inner Chimney (cut and stitch two)
   ⅞" x ⅞"

Ceiling (cut one) 3⅜"x 2⅛"

Bottom (cut one) 3⅜"x 2⅛"

Use five 4" x 4" pieces of plastic canvas for this building. Bold lines on graphs indicate cutting lines. See Suppliers for specialty thread and plastic canvas.

Materials

12 completed designs on clear Plastic
   Canvas 7; matching yarn
3⅜"x 2⅛" unstitched clear Plastic
   Canvas 7 (Ceiling)
3⅜"x 2⅛" unstitched clear Plastic
   Canvas 7 (Bottom)
Fine-tip marker
Polyester stuffing

Directions

1. For each design piece, mark lightly on plastic canvas, following bold lines on graph. Cut carefully.

2. Overcast edges of all building pieces (see Step 2 of color code). Then whipstitch Front, Side, Back and Side together in that order to form a shell. Whipstitch Ceiling to top edge of shell. Whipstitch Roofs on one long edge and then to top of shell/Ceiling. (Place between chimneys, forming a front and back overhang.)

3. To chimney on each side, whipstitch a Chimney Side, Inner Chimney and Chimney Side in that order. Stuff moderately. Whipstitch Bottom to bottom edge to complete building.

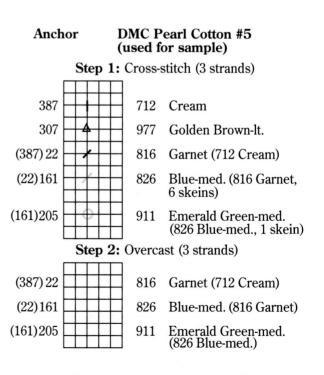

Anchor		DMC Pearl Cotton #5 (used for sample)	
		Step 1: Cross-stitch (3 strands)	
387		712	Cream
307		977	Golden Brown-lt.
(387) 22		816	Garnet (712 Cream)
(22) 161		826	Blue-med. (816 Garnet, 6 skeins)
(161) 205		911	Emerald Green-med. (826 Blue-med., 1 skein)
		Step 2: Overcast (3 strands)	
(387) 22		816	Garnet (712 Cream)
(22) 161		826	Blue-med. (816 Garnet)
(161) 205		911	Emerald Green-med. (826 Blue-med.)

Patriotic Village

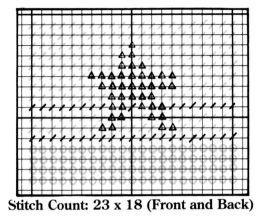

Stitch Count: 23 x 18 (Front and Back)

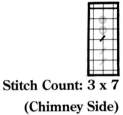

Stitch Count: 3 x 7

(Chimney Side)

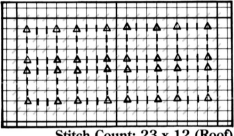

Stitch Count: 23 x 12 (Roof)

Stitch Count: 7 x 6

(Inner Chimney)

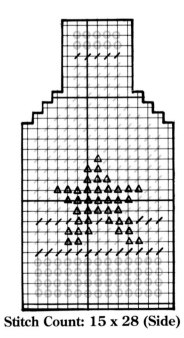

Stitch Count: 15 x 28 (Side)

Smyrna Cross Building

S titched on clear Plastic Canvas 7 over one mesh. Use floss in parentheses for alternate building colors; see photo.

The canvas was cut:

Front (cut and stitch one) 3⅜" x 2¾"

Back (cut and stitch one) 3⅜" x 2¾"

Side (cut and stitch two) 2⅛" x 4" Roof (cut and stitch two) 3½" x 1½"

Chimney Side (cut and stitch four) ½" x ⅞"

Inner Chimney (cut and stitch two) ⅞" x ⅞"

Ceiling (cut one) 3⅜" x 2⅛"

Bottom (cut one) 3⅜" x 2⅛"

Use five 4" x 4" pieces of plastic canvas for one building. Bold lines on graphs indicate cutting lines. See Suppliers for specialty thread and plastic canvas.

Materials

12 completed designs on clear Plastic
   Canvas 7; matching yarn
3⅜"x 2⅛" unstitched clear Plastic
   Canvas 7 (Ceiling)
3⅜"x 2⅛" unstitched clear Plastic
   Canvas 7 (Bottom)
Fine-tip marker
Polyester stuffing

Directions

1. Repeat Steps 1–3 of Directions for Star Building on page 124.

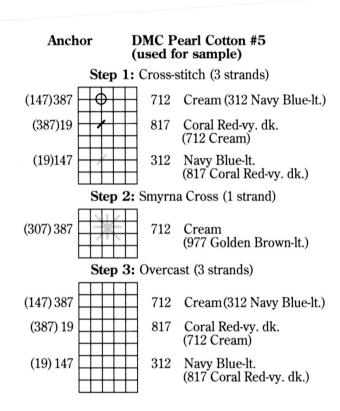

Anchor		DMC Pearl Cotton #5 (used for sample)
Step 1: Cross-stitch (3 strands)		
(147)387		712 Cream (312 Navy Blue-lt.)
(387)19		817 Coral Red-vy. dk. (712 Cream)
(19)147		312 Navy Blue-lt. (817 Coral Red-vy. dk.)
Step 2: Smyrna Cross (1 strand)		
(307) 387		712 Cream (977 Golden Brown-lt.)
Step 3: Overcast (3 strands)		
(147) 387		712 Cream (312 Navy Blue-lt.)
(387) 19		817 Coral Red-vy. dk. (712 Cream)
(19) 147		312 Navy Blue-lt. (817 Coral Red-vy. dk.)

Patriotic Village

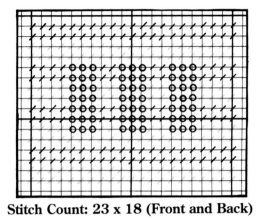

Stitch Count: 23 x 18 (Front and Back)

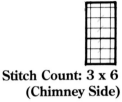

**Stitch Count: 3 x 6
(Chimney Side)**

**Stitch Count: 6 x 6
(Inner Chimney)**

Stitch Count: 23 x 11 (Roof)

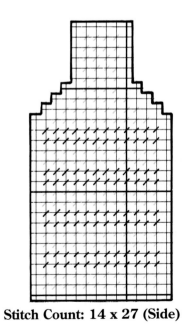

Stitch Count: 14 x 27 (Side)

August Calls

Stitched on Rustico 14, the finished design size is 5" x 7⅛". The fabric was cut 11" x 14". See March Charm on page 18 for cutout instructions. More than one thread represented by a single symbol on the code and graph indicates blending; note number of strands used.

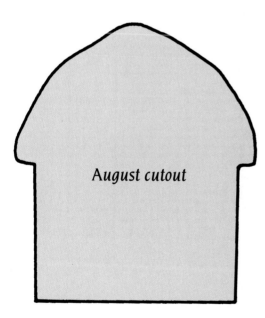

August cutout

Anchor			DMC	(used for sample)

Step 1: Cross-stitch (2 strands)

Anchor	Symbol		DMC	Color
301	∴		744	Yellow-pale
886	•		677	Old Gold-vy. lt.
891	□		676	Old Gold-lt.
307	○		783	Christmas Gold
308	■		976	Golden Brown-med.
323	−	◿	722	Orange Spice-lt.
11	△		350	Coral-med.
13	⊠		347	Salmon-vy. dk.
5975	△		356	Terra Cotta-med.
5968	⊠		355	Terra Cotta-dk.
970	▲		315	Antique Mauve-vy. dk.
921	•	◿	931	Antique Blue-med.
246	○		319	Pistachio Green-vy. dk.
970	⊠		315	Antique Mauve-vy. dk. (1 strand)+
246			319	Pistachio Green-vy. dk. (1 strand)
844	−		3012	Khaki Green-med.
845	●		3011	Khaki Green-dk.

Step 2: Backstitch (1 strand)

Anchor	Symbol	DMC	Color
381	⌐	838	Beige Brown-vy. dk.

130
August Calls

Stitch Count: 70 x 100

Cozy Coverlet

Cozy Coverlet

Design 1

Stitched on Vanessa-Ann Afghan Weave 18 over two threads, the finished design size is 4" x 4". The fabric was cut 48" x 58". See Step 1 of Directions before stitching. See Suppliers for fabric.

Materials

Completed designs on Vanessa-Ann
  Afghan Weave 18
¾ yard of pink fabric; matching thread

Directions

1. The width of the fabric is seven whole blocks plus a half block on each side. The length is eight whole blocks plus a half block on each end. The stitch count of each block is 44 x 44 over two threads and 88 x 88 over one. Begin stitching in center of each block.

2. Trim design piece to 45" x 54". From pink fabric, cut 2¼"-wide bias strips, piecing as needed to equal 5½ yards.

3. Using ½" seam allowance, sew bias to right side of design piece, mitering corners. Fold bias double to wrong side, making a ⅝"-wide binding. Slipstitch in place, over stitching line.

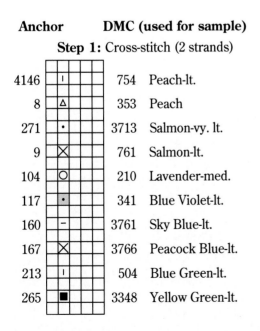

Anchor		DMC (used for sample)	
Step 1: Cross-stitch (2 strands)			
4146	ı	754	Peach-lt.
8	∆	353	Peach
271	•	3713	Salmon-vy. lt.
9	⊠	761	Salmon-lt.
104	○	210	Lavender-med.
117	•	341	Blue Violet-lt.
160	−	3761	Sky Blue-lt.
167	⊠	3766	Peacock Blue-lt.
213	ı	504	Blue Green-lt.
265	■	3348	Yellow Green-lt.

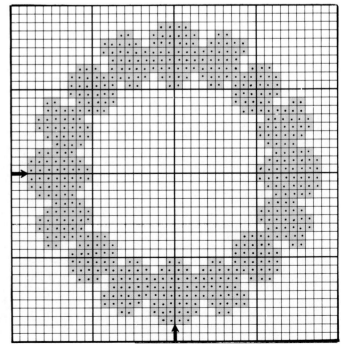

Stitch Count: 36 x 36 (Design 1)

Design 2

Stitched on Vanessa-Ann Afghan Weave 18 over two threads, the finished design size is 4½" x 4½". The fabric was cut 48" x 58". See Step 1 of Directions before stitching. See Suppliers for fabric.

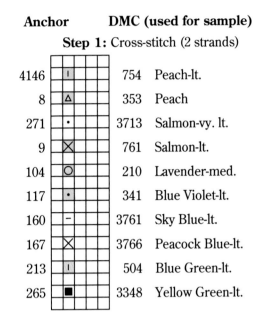

Anchor		DMC (used for sample)	
Step 1: Cross-stitch (2 strands)			
4146	I	754	Peach-lt.
8	△	353	Peach
271	·	3713	Salmon-vy. lt.
9	✕	761	Salmon-lt.
104	○	210	Lavender-med.
117	·	341	Blue Violet-lt.
160	–	3761	Sky Blue-lt.
167	✕	3766	Peacock Blue-lt.
213	I	504	Blue Green-lt.
265	■	3348	Yellow Green-lt.

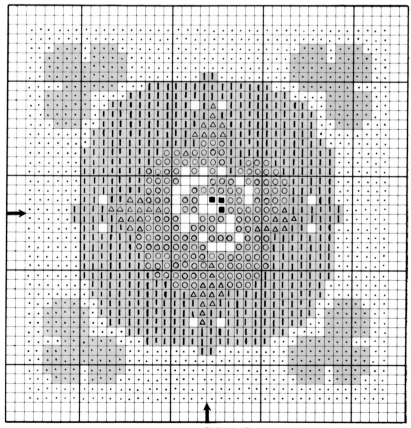

Stitch Count: 40 x 40 (Design 2)

Cozy Coverlet

Design 3

Stitched on Vanessa-Ann Afghan Weave 18, the finished design size is 4½" x 4½". The fabric was cut 48" x 58". See Step 1 of Directions before stitching. See Suppliers for fabric.

Anchor		DMC (used for sample)	
Step 1: Cross-stitch (2 strands)			
4146	I	754	Peach-lt.
8	△	353	Peach
271	•	3713	Salmon-vy. lt.
9	⊠	761	Salmon-lt.
104	○	210	Lavender-med.
117	•	341	Blue Violet-lt.
160	−	3761	Sky Blue-lt.
167	⊠	3766	Peacock Blue-lt.
213	I	504	Blue Green-lt.
265	■	3348	Yellow Green-lt.

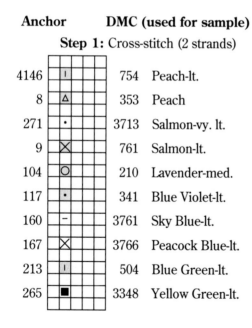

135
Cozy Coverlet

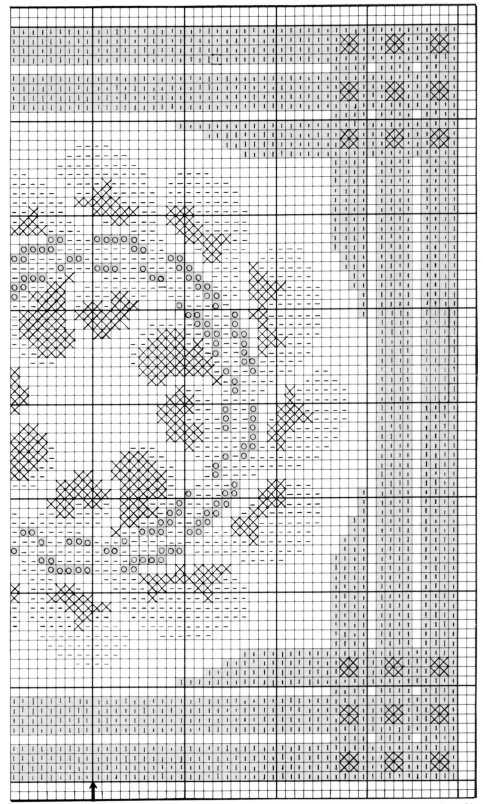

Stitch Count: 80 x 80 (Design 3)

Autumn

Autumn's chill in the air draws
us back inside as we
refocus our attention on
hearth and home.
This is the season for giving
thanks, with a little time set
aside for Halloween highjinks!
The projects in this section
reflect a blend of home
and harvest motifs, including
holiday decorations and
wonderful housewarming gifts.
Fall is an inspirational
source of color and texture, as
you'll see in the rich harvest
tones and smokey shades
featured in this collection
of projects.

Autumn Banner

Stitched on white Country Aida 7, the finished design size is 14" x 32⅛". The fabric was cut 20" x 45". See Suppliers for specialty thread and fabric.

Materials

Completed design on white Country Aida 7; matching thread
2½ yards of coordinating fabric; matching thread
1¼ yards of fleece
1¼ yards of fusible interfacing
2⅜ yards of large cording
16½" length of 1¼"-wide wooden closet rod
Two 1½" x 4½" wooden finials
Acrylic paints
Paintbrush
Glue

Directions
All seams are ¼".

1. Complete Steps 1–5 of Directions for Spring Banner on page 12.

Paternayan Persian Yarn
(used for sample)

Step 1: Cross-stitch (1 strand)

·	⁄·	754	Old Gold
▲	◢	726	Autumn Yellow-lt.
U		803	Marigold
▬		811	Sunrise-dk.
△		832	Bittersweet-med.
⊠		831	Bittersweet-dk.
☐		844	Salmon-lt.
∴		843	Salmon
−		842	Salmon-med.
☐		970	Christmas Red-med.
⁄	◢	969	Christmas Red-dk.
U		940	Cranberry-vy. dk.
·	◢	332	Lavender
−	∠	311	Grape-dk.
◯		322	Plum
⊠		321	Plum-dk.
☐		663	Pine Green
∴	◢	602	Forest Green
△	◢	694	Loden Green-lt.
■		693	Loden Green
·		652	Olive Green
◯		651	Olive Green-dk.
⊠		497	Wicker Brown
⁄	◢	495	Wicker Brown-dk.
⁞		412	Earth Brown-med.
◯	◢	411	Earth Brown-dk.
●		410	Earth Brown-vy. dk.

Step 2: Backstitch (1 strand)

	693	Loden Green (lime)
	495	Wicker Brown-dk. (pineapple)
	410	Earth Brown-vy. dk. (all else)

Autumn Banner

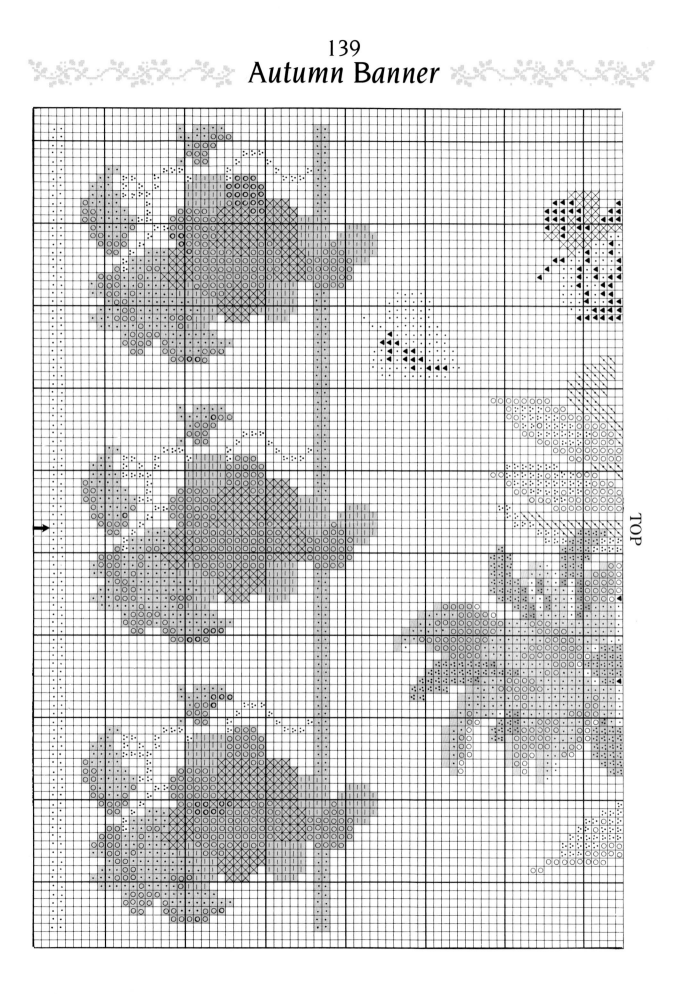

TOP

Autumn Banner

TOP

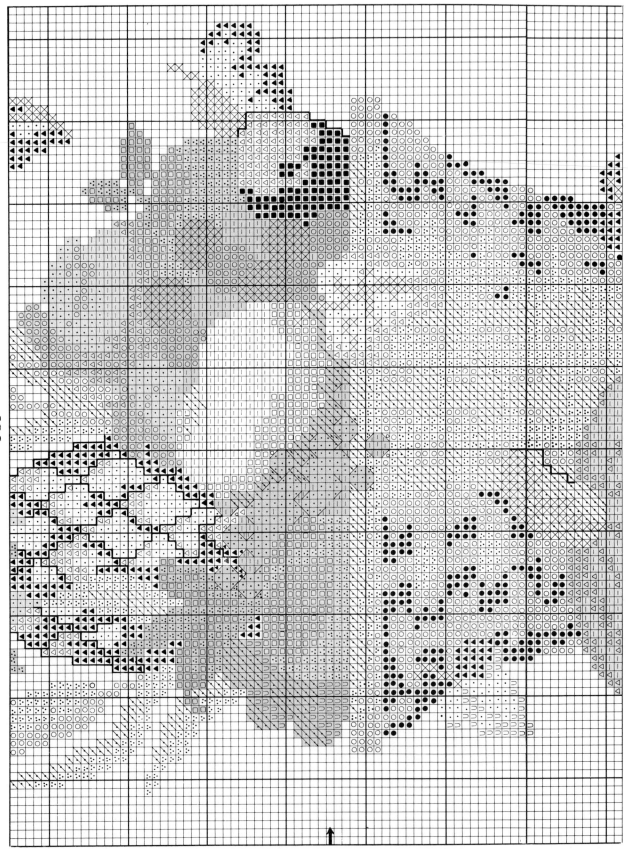

Autumn Banner

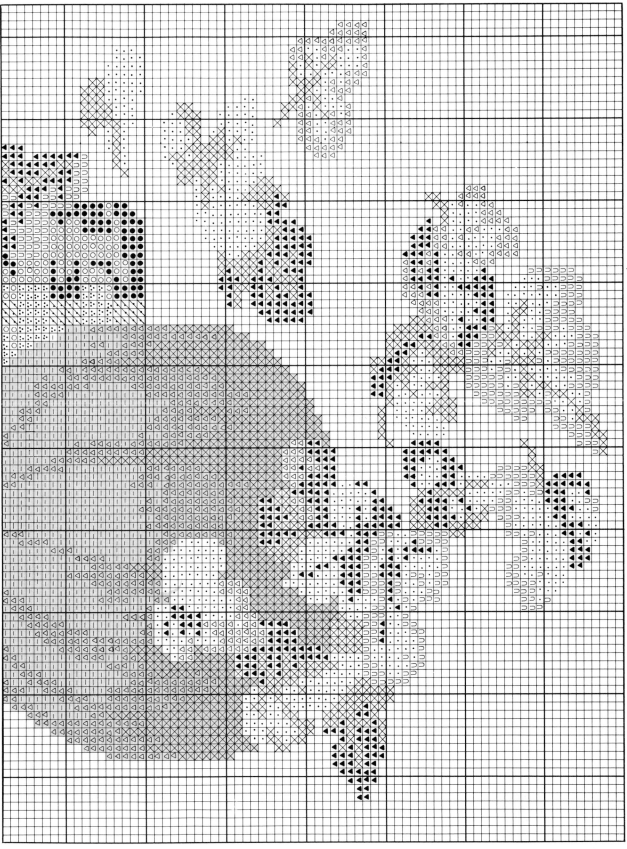

TOP

Stitch Count: 98 x 225

September Majesty

Stitched on cream Murano 30 over two threads, the finished design size is 4⅝" x 6⅝". The fabric was cut 11" x 13". See March Charm on page 18 for cutout instructions.

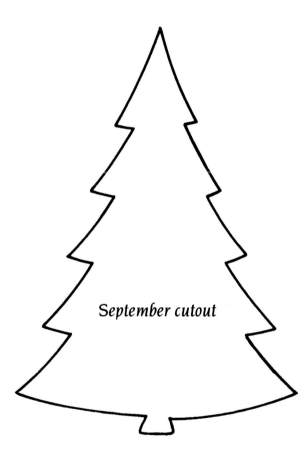

September cutout

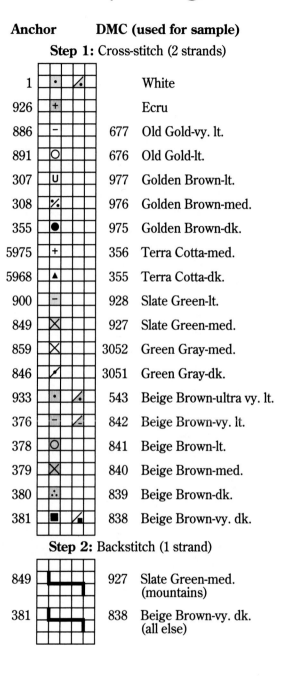

Anchor			DMC (used for sample)	

Step 1: Cross-stitch (2 strands)

Anchor			DMC	
1	·	⁄		White
926	+			Ecru
886	–		677	Old Gold-vy. lt.
891	O		676	Old Gold-lt.
307	U		977	Golden Brown-lt.
308	⁒		976	Golden Brown-med.
355	●		975	Golden Brown-dk.
5975	+		356	Terra Cotta-med.
5968	▲		355	Terra Cotta-dk.
900	–		928	Slate Green-lt.
849	✕		927	Slate Green-med.
859	✕		3052	Green Gray-med.
846	⁄		3051	Green Gray-dk.
933	·	⁄	543	Beige Brown-ultra vy. lt.
376	–	⁄	842	Beige Brown-vy. lt.
378	O		841	Beige Brown-lt.
379	✕		840	Beige Brown-med.
380	∴		839	Beige Brown-dk.
381	■	◢	838	Beige Brown-vy. dk.

Step 2: Backstitch (1 strand)

Anchor		DMC	
849		927	Slate Green-med. (mountains)
381		838	Beige Brown-vy. dk. (all else)

September Majesty

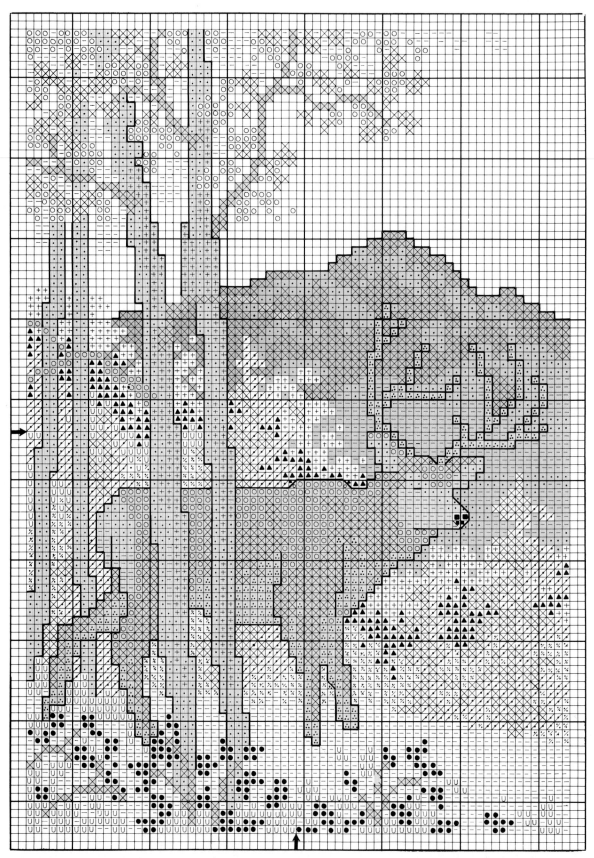

Stitch Count: 70 x 100

Bath Sachets

Heart Design

Stitched on Glenshee Egyptian Cotton Quality D 26 over two threads, the finished design size is 1¼" x ⅞" for each motif. The fabric was cut 12" x 4". See Step 1 of Directions before stitching. See Suppliers for fabric.

Materials
for each design

Completed design on Glenshee Egyptian
   Cotton Quality D 26
⅛ yard of green brocade fabric; matching
   thread
⅝ yard of ¼"-wide rose trim; matching
   thread
Two ⅝"-wide ready-to-cover shank buttons
Polyester stuffing
1½ cups of potpourri
Long sharp needle

Directions
for each design
All seams are ¼".

1. Center motif vertically, stitching repeats to fill horizontal measurement. Leave 1" unstitched at each end. Heavy lines on graph indicate placement of additional motifs.

2. Trim design piece to measure 9½" x 2½" with design centered. Cut two 9½" x 2½" pieces of brocade fabric. Cut trim into two 9½" lengths.

3. With right sides facing and raw edges aligned, stitch one long edge of one fabric piece to one long edge of design piece; repeat to attach remaining fabric piece and design piece edges. With right sides facing and seams aligned, match short raw edges and stitch together to form a tube.

4. Fold under ¼" around one end of tube and sew a gathering stitch. Gather tightly and secure thread. Stuff moderately, adding potpourri to center. Repeat for remaining end. Slipstitch trim over long seams joining fabric to design piece.

5. For sachet shown in foreground of photo, stitch from one gathered end to the other through center of sachet with long needle.

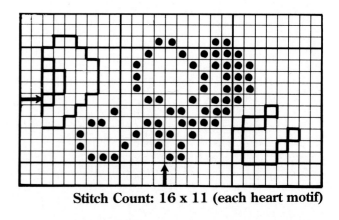

Stitch Count: 16 x 11 (each heart motif)

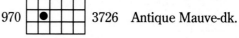

Anchor		DMC (used for sample)
Step 1: Cross-stitch (2 strands)		
970	●	3726 Antique Mauve-dk.

Take six stitches through center, pulling tightly each time to shape sachet; secure thread.

6. Cover shank buttons, following manufacturer's instructions, and tack securely to gathered ends.

Floral Design

Stitched on Glenshee Egyptian Cotton Quality D 26 over two threads, the finished design size is 2½" x 1¾" for each motif. The fabric was cut 13" x 5". See Step 1 of Directions on page 146 before stitching. See Suppliers for fabric.

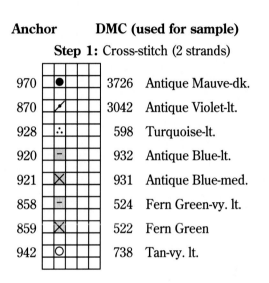

Anchor		DMC (used for sample)	
	Step 1: Cross-stitch (2 strands)		
970	●	3726	Antique Mauve-dk.
870	╱	3042	Antique Violet-lt.
928	∴	598	Turquoise-lt.
920	−	932	Antique Blue-lt.
921	✕	931	Antique Blue-med.
858	−	524	Fern Green-vy. lt.
859	✕	522	Fern Green
942	○	738	Tan-vy. lt.

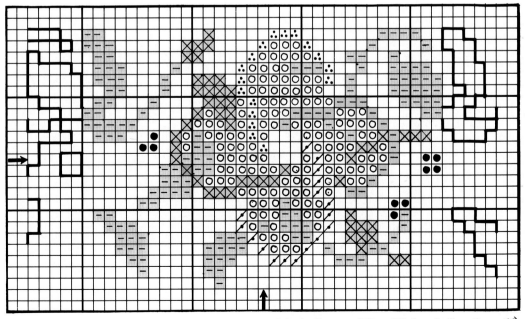

Stitch Count: 33 x 23 (each floral motif)

Welcome

Stitched on wisteria Aida 14, the finished design size is 17¼" x 10½". The fabric was cut 24" x 17". More than one thread represented by a single symbol on the code and graph indicates blending; note the number of strands used. See Suppliers for specialty thread, beads and fabric.

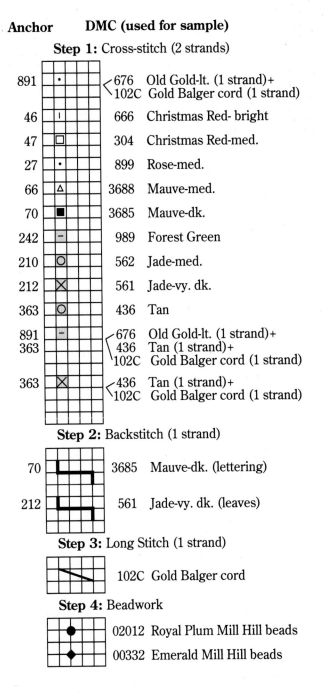

Anchor   DMC (used for sample)

Step 1: Cross-stitch (2 strands)

891	·	< 676	Old Gold-lt. (1 strand)+
		102C	Gold Balger cord (1 strand)
46	I	666	Christmas Red- bright
47	□	304	Christmas Red-med.
27	·	899	Rose-med.
66	△	3688	Mauve-med.
70	■	3685	Mauve-dk.
242	−	989	Forest Green
210	O	562	Jade-med.
212	X	561	Jade-vy. dk.
363	O	436	Tan
891	−	< 676	Old Gold-lt. (1 strand)+
363		436	Tan (1 strand)+
		102C	Gold Balger cord (1 strand)
363	X	< 436	Tan (1 strand)+
		102C	Gold Balger cord (1 strand)

Step 2: Backstitch (1 strand)

| 70 | | 3685 | Mauve-dk. (lettering) |
| 212 | | 561 | Jade-vy. dk. (leaves) |

Step 3: Long Stitch (1 strand)

| | | 102C | Gold Balger cord |

Step 4: Beadwork

| | ● | 02012 | Royal Plum Mill Hill beads |
| | ◆ | 00332 | Emerald Mill Hill beads |

Welcome

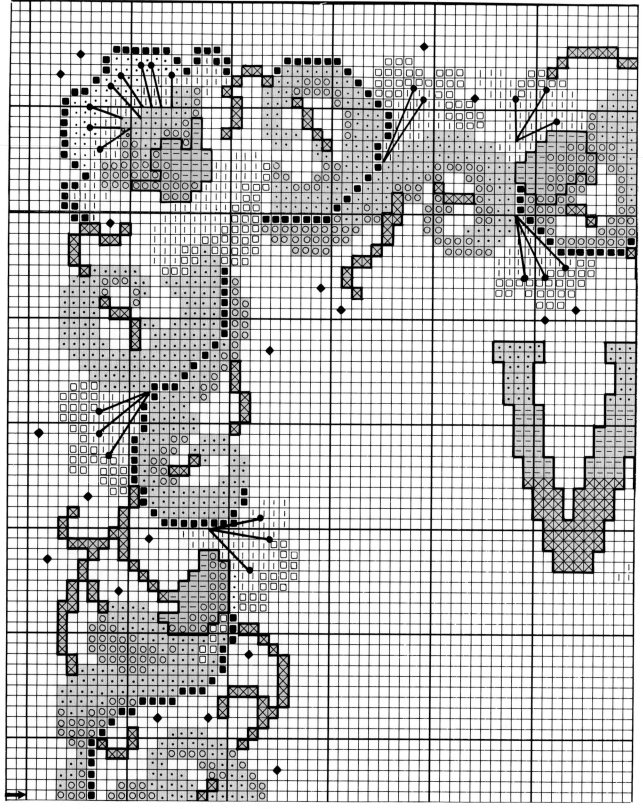

Top left of design

Top center of design

Top center of design

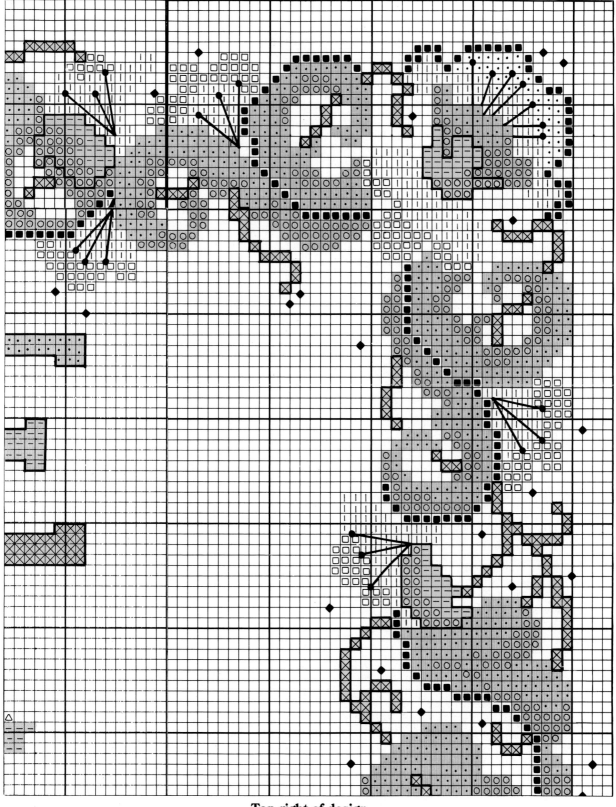

Top right of design

Welcome

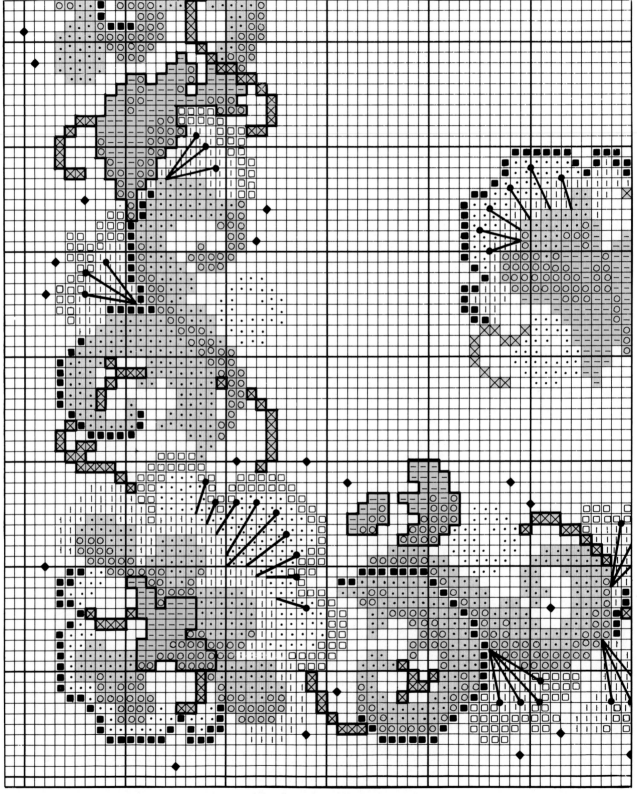

Bottom left of design

Welcome

Bottom center of design

Welcome

Bottom center of design

Welcome

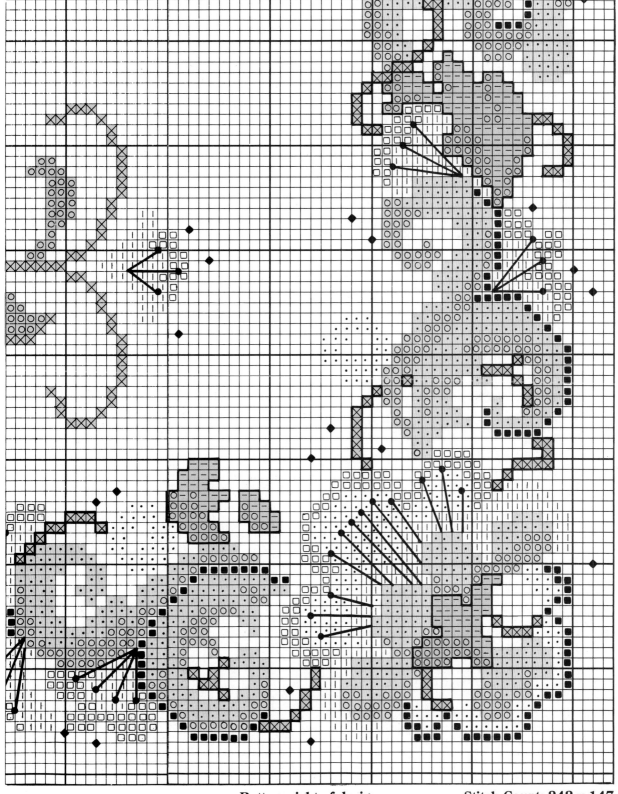

Bottom right of design   **Stitch Count: 242 x 147**

Grandma's Sewing Box

Stitched on bone Tula 10, the finished design size is 13" x 10¾". The fabric was cut 17" x 15". See Suppliers for specialty thread.

Materials

Completed design on bone Tula 10; matching thread
Sewing box (see Suppliers)
Acrylic paints
Paintbrushes
Sponges
Stencils

Directions

1. The graph on pages 160 and 161 represents the left half of the design. Using arrows to find center, begin stitching in center of fabric to complete left half. Then, without turning fabric, turn book upside down, stitching right half. Some symbols will be upside down.

2. Paint box with acrylic paints as desired. Allow to dry.

3. To complete model, zigzag outer edges of design piece, center and staple over insert; place in lid.

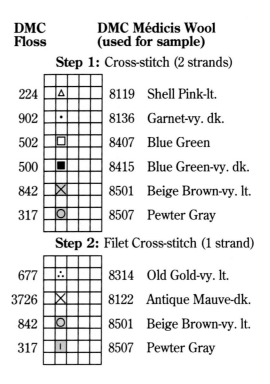

DMC Floss		DMC Médicis Wool (used for sample)	
Step 1: Cross-stitch (2 strands)			
224	△	8119	Shell Pink-lt.
902	•	8136	Garnet-vy. dk.
502	□	8407	Blue Green
500	■	8415	Blue Green-vy. dk.
842	⊠	8501	Beige Brown-vy. lt.
317	○	8507	Pewter Gray
Step 2: Filet Cross-stitch (1 strand)			
677	∴	8314	Old Gold-vy. lt.
3726	⊠	8122	Antique Mauve-dk.
842	○	8501	Beige Brown-vy. lt.
317	I	8507	Pewter Gray

Grandma's Sewing Box

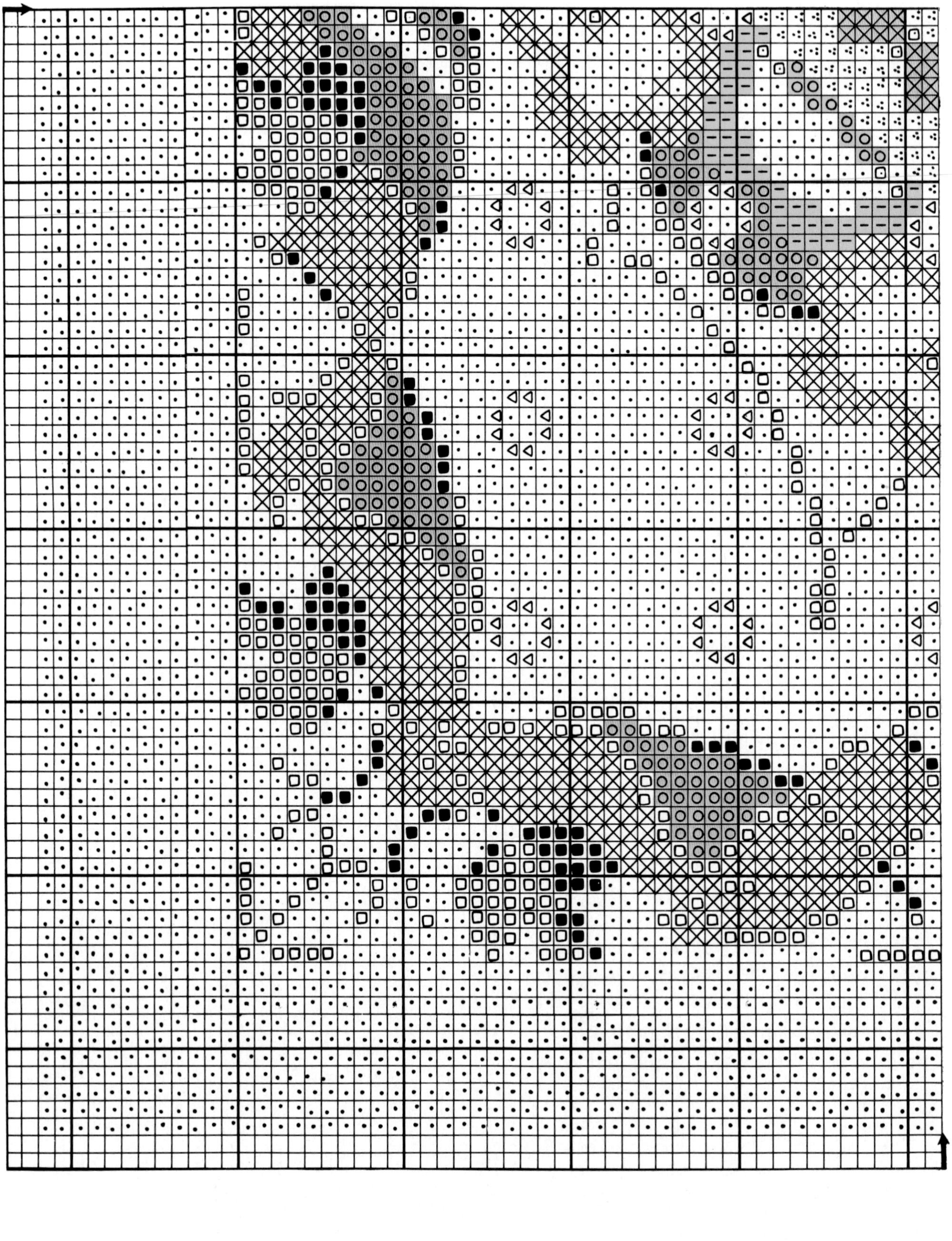

Grandma's Sewing Box

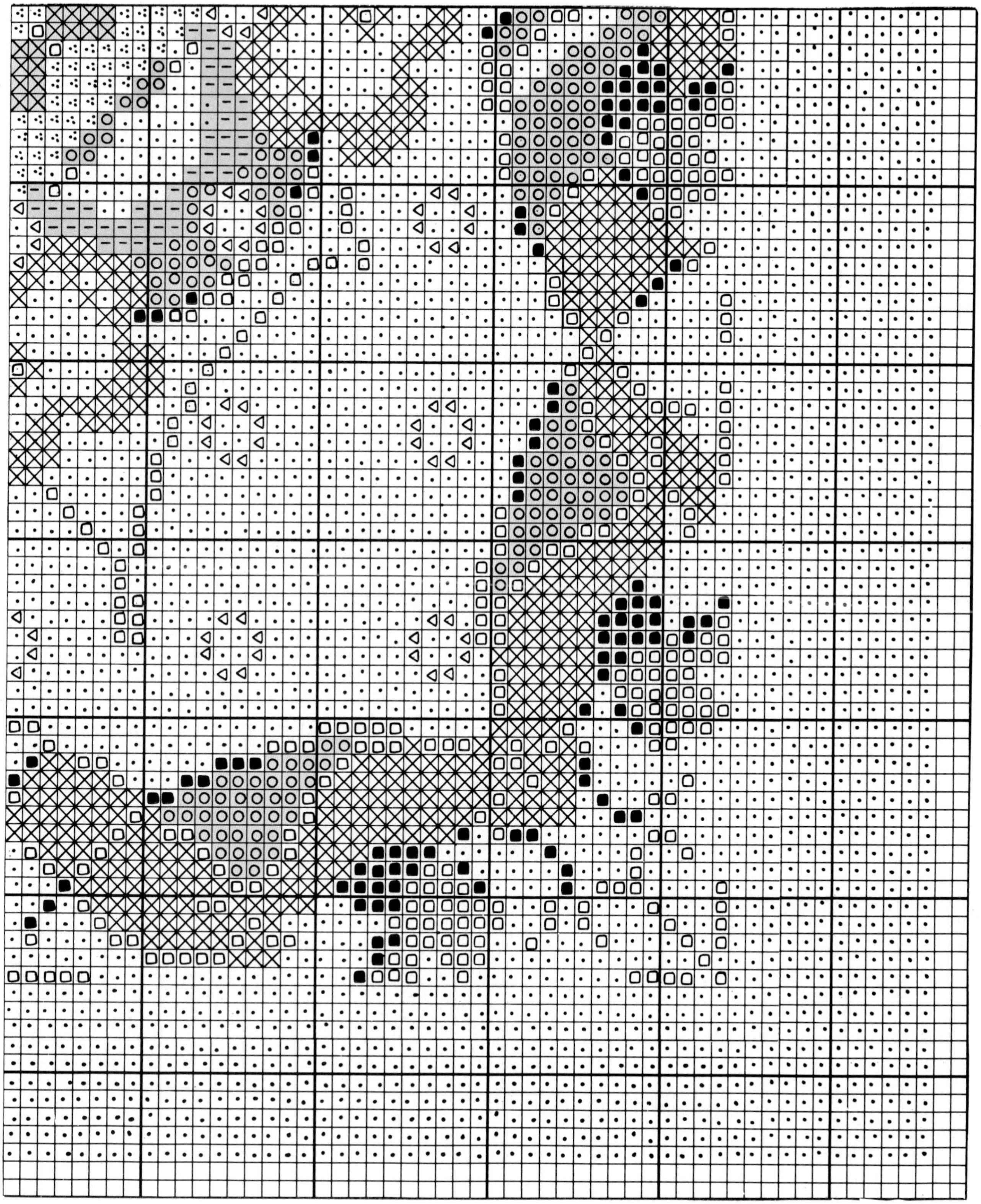

Stitch Count: 130 x 108 (Whole design)

October Wonder

Stitched on amaretto Murano 30 over two threads, the finished design size is 4⅝" x 6⅝". The fabric was cut 11" x 13". See March Charm on page 18 for cutout instructions.

October cutout

Anchor			DMC	(used for sample)
Step 1: Cross-stitch (2 strands)				
387	O	◢	712	Cream
4146	◙	◢	754	Peach-lt.
323	◢	◢	722	Orange Spice-lt.
324	□		721	Orange Spice-med.
326	▲		720	Orange Spice-dk.
20	·		498	Christmas Red-dk.
969	●		316	Antique Mauve-med.
970	△		3726	Antique Mauve-dk.
920	I	◢	932	Antique Blue-lt. (1 strand)
921	☒	◢	931	Antique Blue-med.
922	O		930	Antique Blue-dk.
900	∴		928	Slate Green-lt.
844	·	◢	3012	Khaki Green-med.
380	O	◢	839	Beige Brown-dk.
400	☒		414	Steel Gray-dk.
Step 2: Backstitch (1 strand)				
922			930	Antique Blue-dk. (letters)
382			3371	Black Brown (numbers)
380			839	Beige Brown-dk. (all else)

Stitch Count: 70 x 100

Treat Box

Treat Box

Stitched on cream Murano 30 over two threads, the finished design size is 10⅛" x 7⅛". The fabric was cut 17" x 14".

Materials

Completed design on cream Murano 30; matching thread
Scrap of black pin dot fabric
Scrap each of burgundy, rust and gold fabric
17" x 12" piece of fleece
Scrap of fusing material
17" x 12" piece of mat board
1 yard of ⅜"-wide black satin ribbon
1 yard of ⅛"-wide orange satin ribbon
½ yard of ⅝"-wide rust satin ribbon
Wooden box (see Suppliers)
Acrylic paints: dusty orange, gray and blue
Sponges
Paintbrushes
Tracing paper
Dressmaker's pen
Glue
Hot glue gun and glue

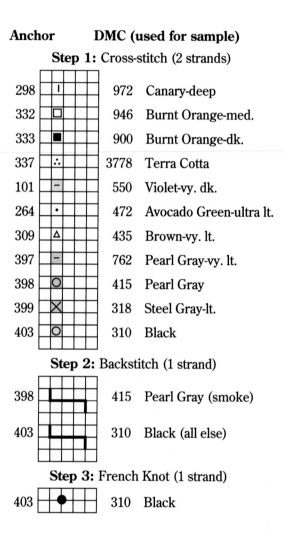

Anchor		DMC (used for sample)	
Step 1: Cross-stitch (2 strands)			
298	I	972	Canary-deep
332	□	946	Burnt Orange-med.
333	■	900	Burnt Orange-dk.
337	∴	3778	Terra Cotta
101	−	550	Violet-vy. dk.
264	•	472	Avocado Green-ultra lt.
309	△	435	Brown-vy. lt.
397	−	762	Pearl Gray-vy. lt.
398	○	415	Pearl Gray
399	✕	318	Steel Gray-lt.
403	○	310	Black
Step 2: Backstitch (1 strand)			
398		415	Pearl Gray (smoke)
403		310	Black (all else)
Step 3: French Knot (1 strand)			
403	●	310	Black

Treat Box

Directions

1. Paint box with acrylic paints as desired; see photo. Allow to dry.

2. Make patterns for moon and stars. Cut one moon from pin dot fabric and fusing material. Cut one large star each from burgundy and rust fabric and fusing material. Cut one small star each from burgundy, rust and gold fabric and fusing material. Set aside.

3. Trim design piece to 17" x 12". Cut black and orange ribbon each into two equal lengths. Glue a black ribbon length horizontally and parallel to last row of stitching at bottom of design piece. Glue an orange ribbon length centered on black ribbon. Glue rust ribbon length below black and orange ribbon. Glue the remaining black ribbon centered on rust ribbon. Glue remaining orange ribbon below rust ribbon; see photo.

4. Following manufacturer's instructions for fusing, fuse moon and stars on design piece as desired; see photo.

5. To complete box lid, glue fleece to mat board. Zigzag outer edges of design piece, center over fleece, fold and glue to back. Glue to box lid top.

Small Star

Moon

Large Star

Treat Box

Treat Box

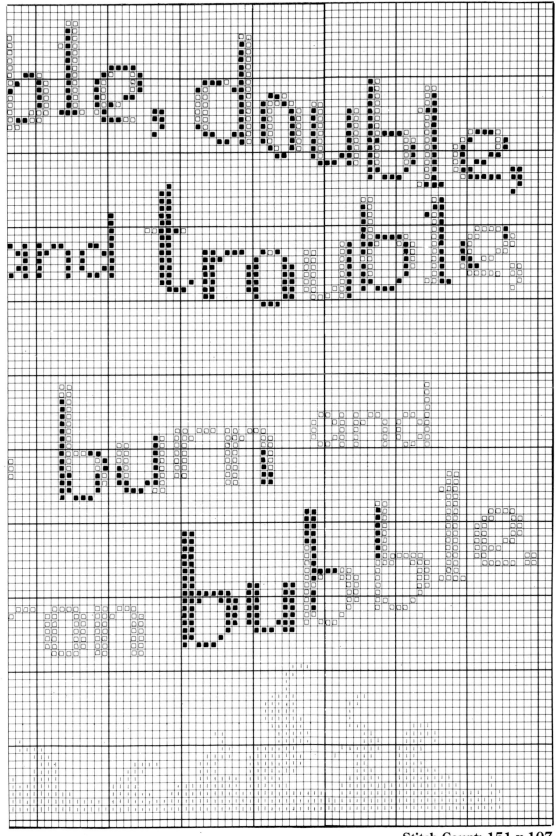

Stitch Count: 151 x 107

Harvest Coasters

Stitched on cream Hardanger 22 over two threads, the finished design size is 3⅛" x 3⅛" for each design. The fabric was cut 6" x 6" for each.

Materials
(for one coaster)

Completed design on cream Hardanger 22
¼ yard of blue pin dot fabric; matching
  thread
¼ cup of crushed potpourri
6" square of fleece
Dressmaker's pen

Directions
All seams are ¼".

1. Trim design to 3½" square. From pin dot fabric, cut four 1¾" x 6½" pieces for border, one 6" square for back, and 1¼"-wide bias strips, piecing as needed to make ¾ yard for binding. Center design piece on fleece, marking corners. Using marks, make a 3" square on fleece center and cut out.

2. To attach border strips to design, mark center of one long edge of each border strip and center of each design edge. With right sides facing, match marks and stitch each border strip to design, stitching to within ¼" of each corner. Backstitch, mitering each corner. Press seams toward strip.

3. Layer coaster back (wrong side up), fleece and coaster front (wrong side down) with raw edges aligned. Stitch in-the-ditch of the design, leaving one edge open. Insert crushed potpourri into center design square. Stitch opening closed.

4. With right sides facing and raw edges aligned, pin binding to border edge. Stitch, mitering each corner.

5. Fold binding ¼" double to wrong side. Slipstitch in place, covering stitching line and mitering corners.

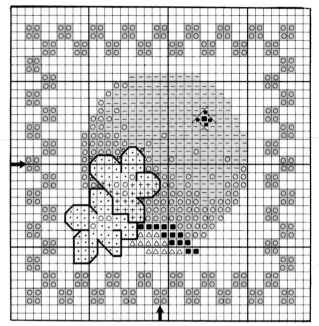

Stitch Count: 34 x 34 (Orange)

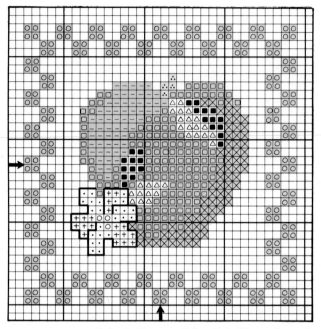

Stitch Count: 34 x 34 (Strawberry)

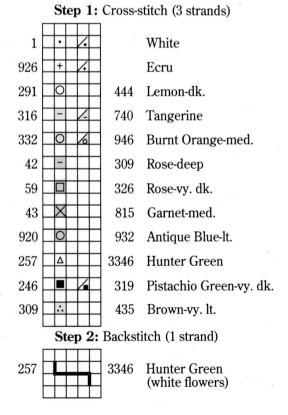

Anchor   **DMC (used for sample)**

Step 1: Cross-stitch (3 strands)

Anchor			DMC	Color
1	·	⁄		White
926	+	⁄		Ecru
291	O		444	Lemon-dk.
316	–	⁄	740	Tangerine
332	O	⁄	946	Burnt Orange-med.
42	–		309	Rose-deep
59	□		326	Rose-vy. dk.
43	✕		815	Garnet-med.
920	O		932	Antique Blue-lt.
257	△		3346	Hunter Green
246	■	⁄	319	Pistachio Green-vy. dk.
309	∴		435	Brown-vy. lt.

Step 2: Backstitch (1 strand)

		DMC	Color
257		3346	Hunter Green (white flowers)

Home Sweet Home

Home Sweet Home

Stitched on cream Murano 30 over two threads, the finished design size is 12⅞" x 8⅝". The fabric was cut 19" x 15". See Suppliers for beads.

Anchor **DMC (used for sample)**

Step 1: Cross-stitch (2 strands)

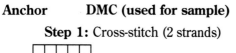

886	677	Old Gold-vy. lt.
8	353	Peach
10	352	Coral-lt.

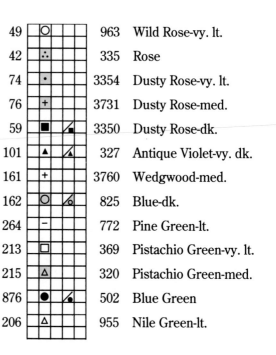

49	963	Wild Rose-vy. lt.
42	335	Rose
74	3354	Dusty Rose-vy. lt.
76	3731	Dusty Rose-med.
59	3350	Dusty Rose-dk.
101	327	Antique Violet-vy. dk.
161	3760	Wedgwood-med.
162	825	Blue-dk.
264	772	Pine Green-lt.
213	369	Pistachio Green-vy. lt.
215	320	Pistachio Green-med.
876	502	Blue Green
206	955	Nile Green-lt.

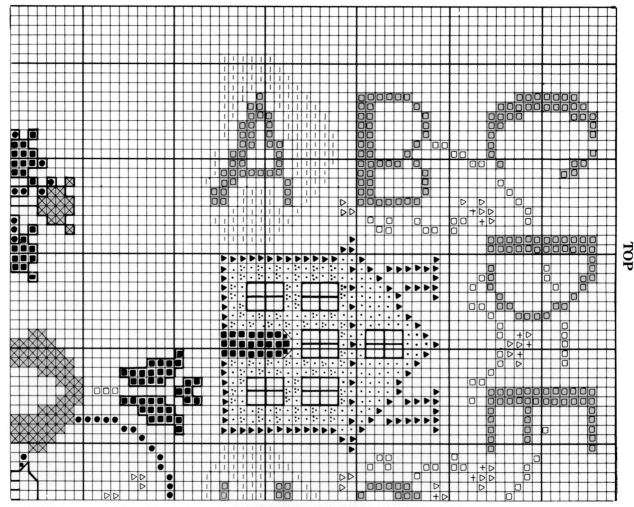

Top left of design

TOP

Home Sweet Home

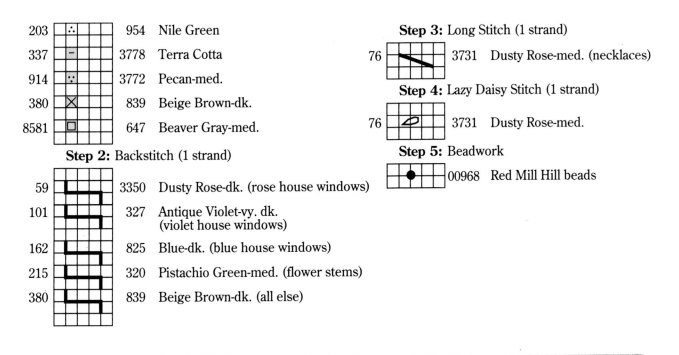

203		954	Nile Green
337		3778	Terra Cotta
914		3772	Pecan-med.
380		839	Beige Brown-dk.
8581		647	Beaver Gray-med.

Step 2: Backstitch (1 strand)

59		3350	Dusty Rose-dk. (rose house windows)
101		327	Antique Violet-vy. dk. (violet house windows)
162		825	Blue-dk. (blue house windows)
215		320	Pistachio Green-med. (flower stems)
380		839	Beige Brown-dk. (all else)

Step 3: Long Stitch (1 strand)

76		3731	Dusty Rose-med. (necklaces)

Step 4: Lazy Daisy Stitch (1 strand)

76		3731	Dusty Rose-med.

Step 5: Beadwork

	00968	Red Mill Hill beads

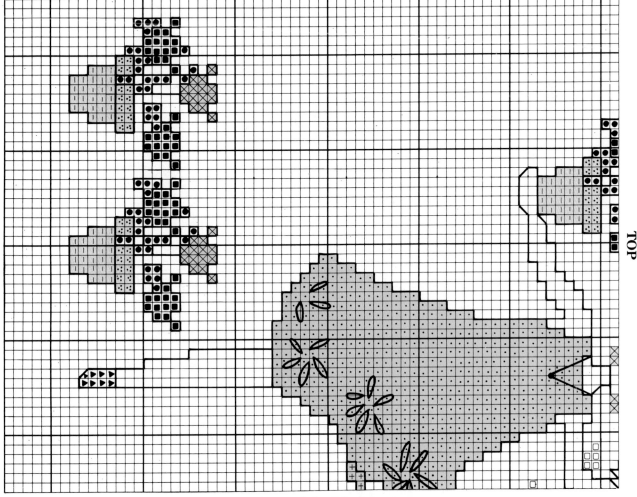

Bottom left of design

Home Sweet Home

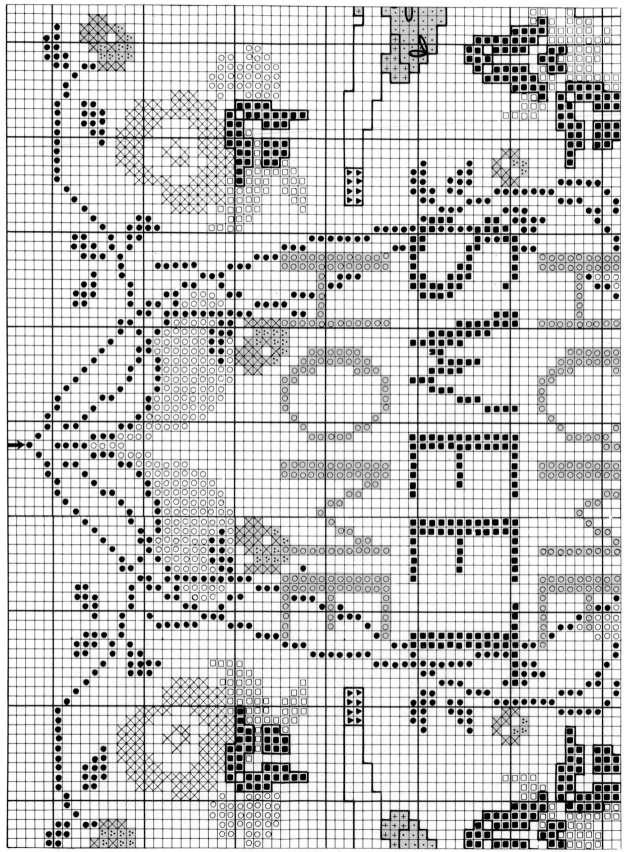

TOP

Bottom center of design

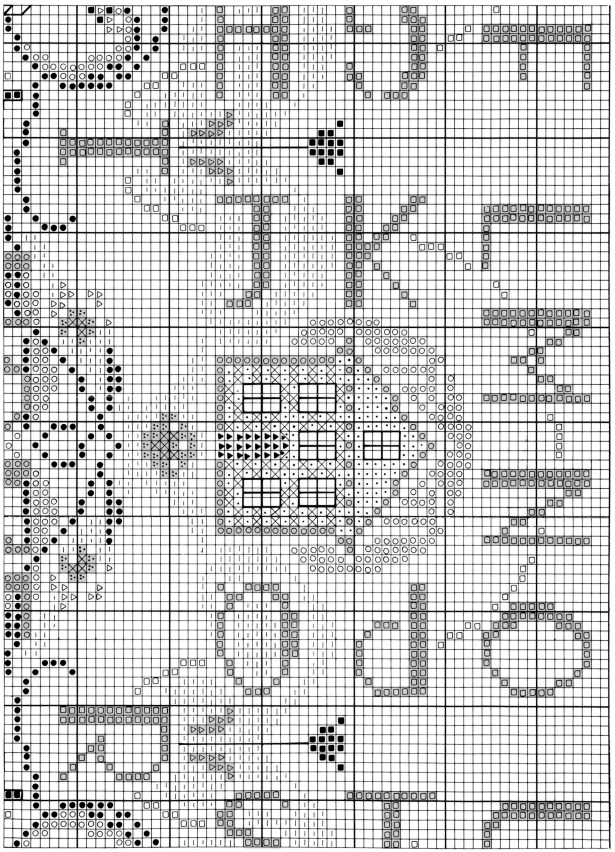

TOP

Top center of design

Home Sweet Home

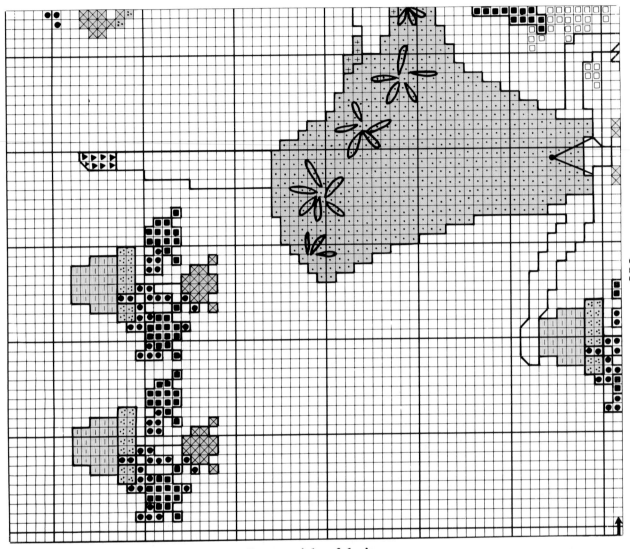

TOP

Bottom right of design

Home Sweet Home

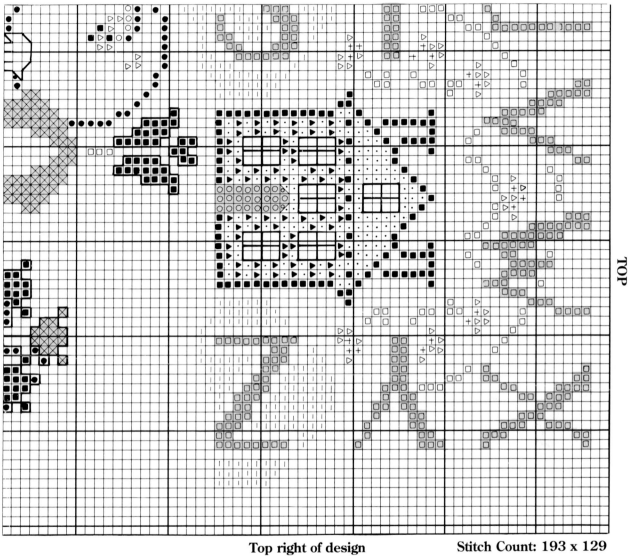

Top right of design

Stitch Count: 193 x 129

TOP

Old Home Place

Stitched on cream Aida 14, the finished design size is 6⅛" x 5⅞". The fabric was cut 13" x 12". Transfer letters desired from alphabet to graph paper, allowing one stitch between letters. Mark placement on fabric and stitch.

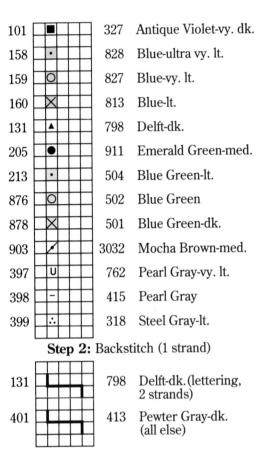

101	■	327	Antique Violet-vy. dk.
158	·	828	Blue-ultra vy. lt.
159	O	827	Blue-vy. lt.
160	✕	813	Blue-lt.
131	▲	798	Delft-dk.
205	●	911	Emerald Green-med.
213	·	504	Blue Green-lt.
876	O	502	Blue Green
878	✕	501	Blue Green-dk.
903	╱	3032	Mocha Brown-med.
397	U	762	Pearl Gray-vy. lt.
398	–	415	Pearl Gray
399	∴	318	Steel Gray-lt.

Step 2: Backstitch (1 strand)

| 131 | | 798 | Delft-dk. (lettering, 2 strands) |
| 401 | | 413 | Pewter Gray-dk. (all else) |

Anchor   **DMC (used for sample)**

Step 1: Cross-stitch (2 strands)

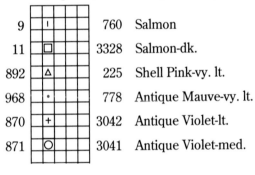

9	ı	760	Salmon
11	□	3328	Salmon-dk.
892	△	225	Shell Pink-vy. lt.
968	·	778	Antique Mauve-vy. lt.
870	+	3042	Antique Violet-lt.
871	O	3041	Antique Violet-med.

Alphabet

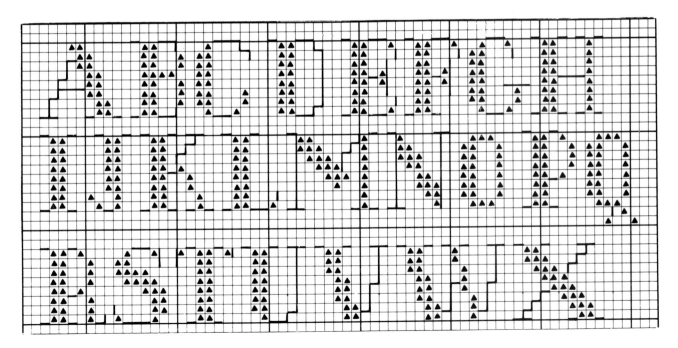

Old Home Place

Stitch Count: 86 x 82

November Harvest

Stitched on cream Murano 30 over two threads, the finished design size is 4⅝" x 6⅝". The fabric was cut 11" x 13". More than one thread represented by a single symbol on the code and graph indicates blending; note the number of strands used. See March Charm on page 18 for cutout instructions.

Anchor			DMC (used for sample)	
			Step 1: Cross-stitch (2 strands)	
306	+		725	Topaz
306 / 264	·	◿	725 / 472	Topaz (1 strand)+ Avocado Green-ultra lt. (1 strand)
8	◿		353	Peach
10	▲	◿	352	Coral-lt.
323	△		722	Orange Spice-lt.
324	U		721	Orange Spice-med.
69	·	◿	3687	Mauve
19	◙		817	Coral Red-vy. dk.
20	●	◿	498	Christmas Red-dk.
43	∴	◿	815	Garnet-med.
98	∴	◿	553	Violet-med.
99	+	◿	552	Violet-dk.
266	✕	◿	3347	Yellow Green-med.
216	○	◿	367	Pistachio Green-dk.
246	■	◿	319	Pistachio Green-vy. dk.
307	I		977	Golden Brown-lt.
308	∴	◿	976	Golden Brown-med.
355	□	◿	975	Golden Brown-dk.

Step 2: Backstitch (1 strand)

Anchor		DMC	
99	▬	552	Violet-dk. (grapes)
266	▬	3347	Yellow Green-med. (pears)
355	▬	975	Golden Brown-dk. (all else)

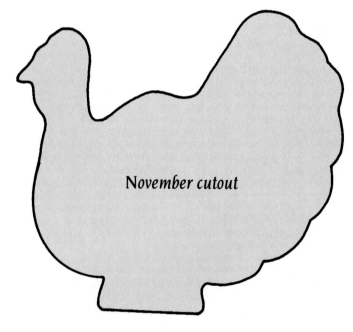

November cutout

November Harvest

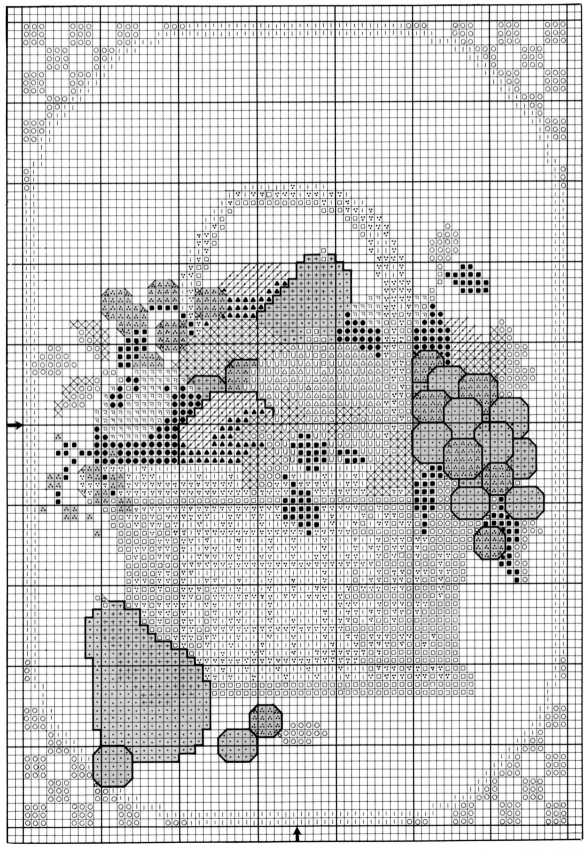

Stitch Count: 70 x 100

Autumn Bands

Flowerpot Band

Stitched on amaretto Murano 30 over two threads, the finished design size is 1⅜" x ¾" for each motif. See Step 1 of Directions before cutting fabric.

Materials

Completed design on amaretto Murano 30; matching thread
1 yard of 1"-wide peach/green variegated wired ribbon
5¼"-high clay flowerpot
Assorted craft flowers, leaves, fruits, nuts
Hot glue gun and glue

Directions
All seams are ¼".

1. Before stitching design, measure around flowerpot lip and add 6" for horizontal measurement. Add 6" to vertical measurement of motif. Cut one unstitched fabric strip to match measurements.

2. Center design vertically and begin stitching first motif 2½" from one short end of fabric. Stitch enough repeats to fill horizontal measurement, leaving 2½" unstitched at opposite end. Heavy lines on graph indicate placement of additional motifs. Measure 1¼" above and below design; trim fabric. Trim 2¼" from each end.

3. With right sides facing and long raw edges aligned, fold design in half. Stitch long edge to make a tube. Turn right side out. Position seam in center back and press.

4. Wrap band around flowerpot with ½" extending below lip. Fold in seam allowance on one end of band. Insert raw edge of other end into folded end. Slipstitch ends together. Glue band to pot.

5. Mark ribbon center, gluing to band seam. Allow a ½" overlap of ribbon to cover bottom edge of band. Glue each half of ribbon around flowerpot, gathering slightly and tying a bow in front. Glue decorations on bow as desired; see photo.

Tray Band

Stitched on amaretto Murano 30 over two threads, the finished design size is 3" x 1½" for each motif. See Step 2 of Directions on page 188 before cutting fabric.

Materials

Completed design on amaretto Murano 30; matching thread
Square wooden tray
Acrylic paints
Paintbrushes

Autumn Bands

Directions
All seams are ¼".

1. Paint tray with acrylic paints as desired. Allow to dry.

2. Before stitching design, measure around tray lip and add 6" for horizontal measurement. Add 6" to vertical measurement of motif. Cut one unstitched fabric strip to match these measurements.

3. To complete tray band, see Steps 2–3 of Directions for flowerpot band on page 187.

4. Wrap band around tray lip. Fold in seam allowance on one end of band. Insert raw edge of other end into folded end. Slipstitch ends together.

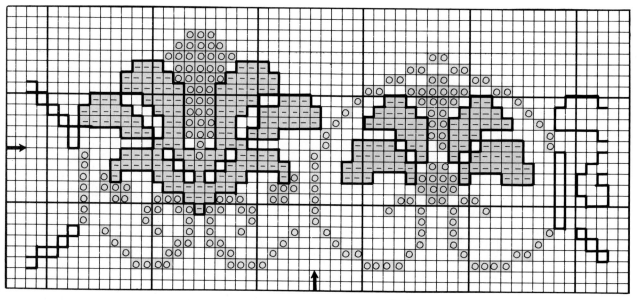

Stitch Count: 22 x 45 (each tray motif)

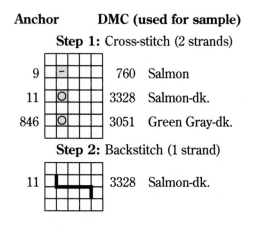

Anchor		DMC (used for sample)	
Step 1: Cross-stitch (2 strands)			
9	−	760	Salmon
11	⊙	3328	Salmon-dk.
846	⊙	3051	Green Gray-dk.
Step 2: Backstitch (1 strand)			
11	▅	3328	Salmon-dk.

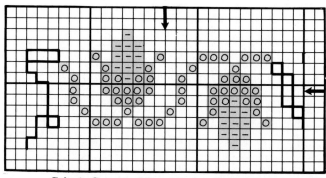

Stitch Count: 20 x 11 (each flowerpot motif)

Sampler Pillow

Sampler Pillow

Stitched on cream Belfast Linen 32 over three threads, the finished design size is 9⅞" x 6¼". The fabric was cut 13" x 10". See Suppliers for beads.

Materials

Completed design on cream Belfast Linen 32
1½ yards of pink/green print fabric; matching thread
½ yard of green print fabric
1 yard of medium cording
1½ yards of large cording
½ yard of fleece
Polyester stuffing

Directions
All seams are ¼".

1. Trim design piece to 10¾" x 7". From green/pink print fabric, cut one 18" x 14" piece for back. Also cut 4"-wide pieces for border, piecing as needed to equal 4½ yards. From green print fabric, cut 1¾"-wide bias strips, piecing as needed to equal 1 yard. Also cut 3"-wide bias strips, piecing as needed to equal 1½ yards. Make 1 yard of medium and 1½ yards of large corded piping. Cut two 18" x 14" pieces of fleece.

2. Stitch medium piping to design piece with right sides facing and raw edges aligned.

Mark center of each edge of design piece and back piece.

3. Join border pieces end-to-end. Sew gathering threads on both long edges. Fold long edges into quarters and mark.

4. Match marks on one long border edge to marks on design piece edges. Gather border to fit design piece, allowing extra fullness at each corner. Stitch.

5. Gather outside border edge enough to lie smoothly. Place design piece over pillow back and slightly round back corners to fit. Using back as pattern, round fleece corners. Pin fleece to wrong side of design piece and back. Zigzag edges. Press as needed to keep smooth.

6. Stitch large piping to back with right sides facing and raw edges aligned.

7. Stitch design piece and back together, matching marks on outside border edge to marks on back and leaving an opening. Turn. Stuff pillow firmly. Slipstitch opening closed.

Sampler Pillow

Anchor   **DMC (used for sample)**

Step 1: Cross-stitch (2 strands)

858   524   Fern Green-vy. lt.

Step 2: Satin Stitch (2 strands)

858   524   Fern Green-vy. lt.

859   523   Fern Green-lt.

859   523   Fern Green-lt.

Step 3: Herringbone Stitch (2 strands)

858   524   Fern Green-vy. lt.
                (stitch over 1/8"
                purple ribbon)

Step 4: Backstitch (2 strands)

859   523   Fern Green-lt.

Step 5: French Knot (1 strand)

        Purple 1/8" silk ribbon

Step 6: Craft Beads

▲   Green (long)

△   Purple

●   Green (round)

Step 7: Mill Hill Beads (3 per stitch)

◆   03020 Dusty Mauve

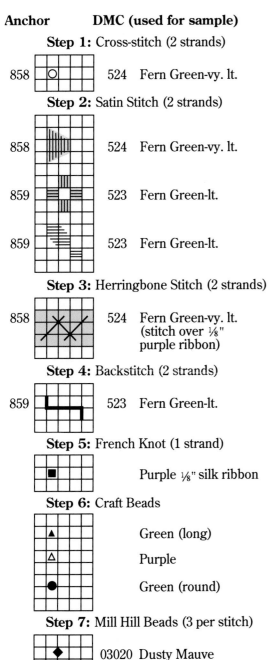

Stitch Count 105 x 67 (Whole design)

Thanksgiving Feast

Table Runner

Materials

2 yards of cream fabric; matching thread
⅛ yard of blue fabric; matching thread
⅛ yard of lavender fabric
Scrap of rust fabric
Scrap of tan fabric
Tracing paper
Dressmaker's pen
Cardboard

Directions
All seams are ¼".

1. Make Templates A, B, C and D.

2. Cut one 13½" x 72" backing piece, one 13½" x 55½" front center piece, two 13½" x 3½" end pieces and eight Template Cs from cream fabric. From blue fabric, cut four 13½" x 1¼" strips, two Template As and 20 Template Bs. From lavender, cut four 13½" x 1¼" strips. From rust, cut 20 Template Bs and eight Template Ds. Cut eight Template As from tan.

3. Join one blue Template B to one rust Template B on long edge; repeat to make 16 sets. Open out and press.

4. To make pieced ends, join one tan Template A, two blue/rust sets, two Template Ds and one blue Template B (**Diagram 1**). Repeat to make four pieced ends.

5. To make center block, join one tan Template A, one blue/rust set and one rust Template B. Repeat to make two rows. Stitch one blue Template A between two blue/rust sets, stitching this row between first two rows (**Diagram 2**). Repeat to make second center block.

6. To complete pieced section, join two pieced ends and one center block to four cream Template Cs (**Diagram 3**). Repeat to make second pieced section.

7. Join one blue strip to one lavender strip on long edges. Repeat to make four strip sets. Join lavender edge to each long edge of each pieced section.

8. Join pieced sections to each end of cream center section. Then join cream end pieces. Trim front; with right sides facing, stitch front to back, leaving an opening. Clip corners. Turn. Slipstitch opening closed.

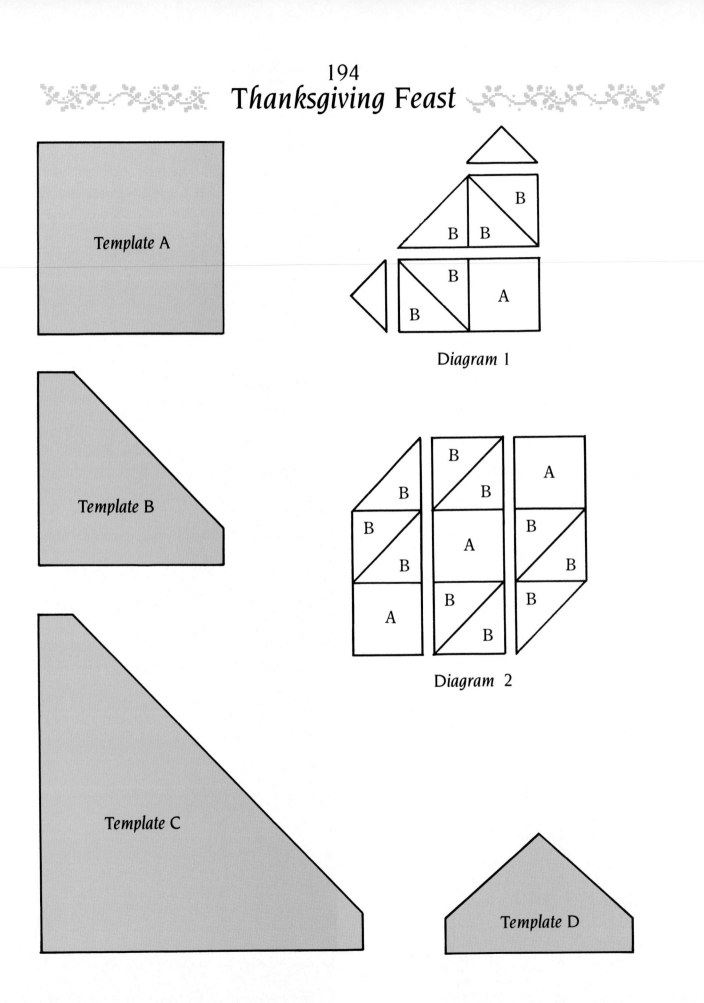

Template A

Template B

Template C

Template D

Diagram 1

Diagram 2

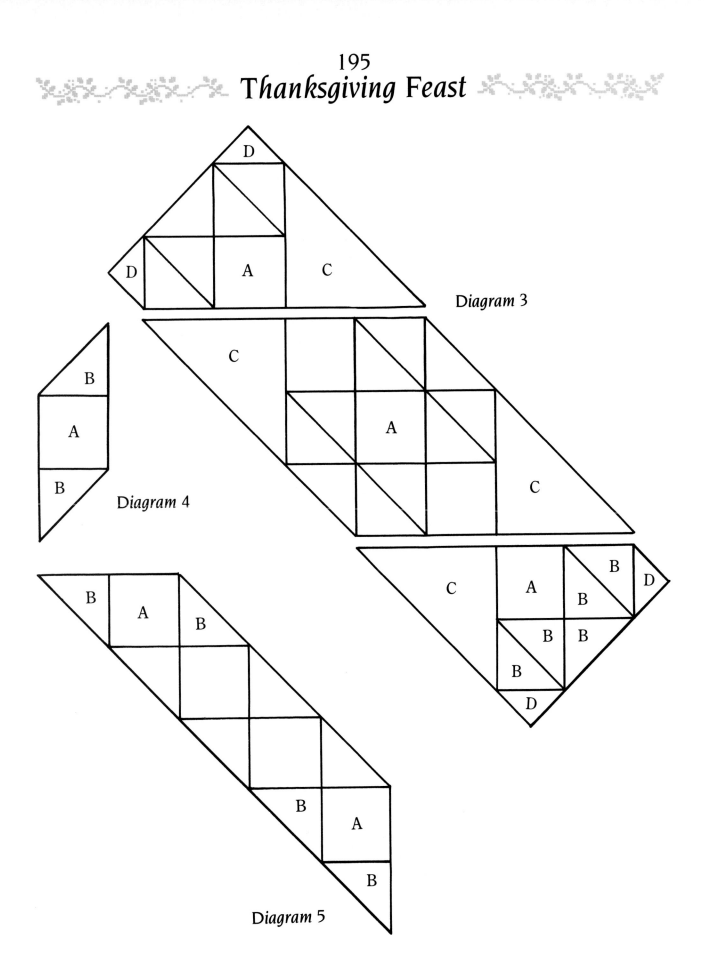

Diagram 3

Diagram 4

Diagram 5

Cornucopia

Stitched on sand Dublin Linen 25, the finished design size is 1¾" x 1⅛" for each motif. The fabric was cut 18" x 5". See Step 1 of Directions below before stitching.

Materials

Completed design on sand Dublin Linen 25; matching thread
⅛ yard of tan fabric
6"-wide wicker cornucopia
Hot glue gun and glue

Directions

1. Center motif vertically, stitching to fill horizontal measurement. Leave ¼" unstitched at each end. Heavy lines on graph indicate placement of additional motifs.

2. Trim design piece to 17" x 2¾" with design centered. Pull threads on long edges to make ⅝"-wide fringe. Set aside.

3. From tan fabric, tear three 1" x 45" strips. Remove cornucopia feet, if needed. Beginning at wide end of cornucopia, glue one strip end to wicker. Wrap strip, gluing as needed, and overlapping. Glue strip ends together as needed, covering entire cornucopia.

4. Wrap design piece around wide end, overlapping on bottom. Fold under top end of design piece; slipstitch securely.

Napkin Set

Stitched on sand Dublin Linen 25, the finished design size is 1¾" x 1⅛" for each motif. The fabric was cut 9" x 5". See Step 1 of Directions for Cornucopia before stitching.

Materials
(for one)

Completed design on sand Dublin Linen 25; matching thread
15" square of cream fabric; matching thread
¼ yard of lavender fabric; matching thread
Scrap of blue fabric
Scrap of rust fabric
Tracing paper
Dressmaker's pen
Cardboard

Directions
All seams are ¼".

1. To make napkin ring, trim design piece to 6½" x 2¾" with design centered. Pull threads on long edges to make ⅝"-wide fringe. Stitch ends together with right sides facing. Turn.

Thanksgiving Feast

2. For napkin, make Templates A and B.

3. Cut four blue Template As. Cut eight rust Template Bs. Cut 1½"-wide bias strips from lavender fabric, piecing as needed to equal 62" for binding.

4. To make pieced section, join blue As and rust Bs in rows (**Diagram 4**). Then join rows, using all pieces (**Diagram 5**).

5. Fold under seam allowance on each long edge of pieced section, placing diagonally across one corner of cream square, aligning raw edges. Slipstitch long edges.

6. With right sides facing, stitch binding to square, mitering corners.

7. Fold binding ¼" double to wrong side and slipstitch in place over stitching line.

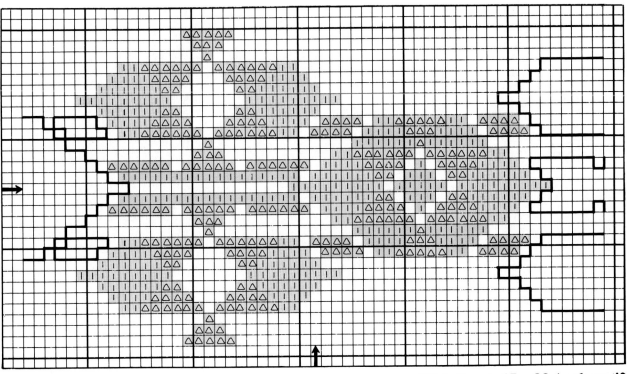

Stitch Count: 45 x 29 (each motif)

Anchor	DMC (used for sample)

Step 1: Cross-stitch (1 strand)

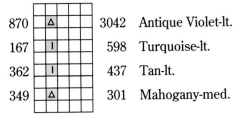

870	△	3042	Antique Violet-lt.
167	I	598	Turquoise-lt.
362	I	437	Tan-lt.
349	△	301	Mahogany-med.

Winter

As winter settles in,
the long, dark days are
interrupted by the
warm glow and sparkling lights
of Christmas festivities.
This section is brimming
with delightful decorations
to dress your home
for the holidays.
You'll also find gifts to celebrate
the most romantic day
of the year--Valentine's Day.
What better way to show your
affection than with
something you've stitched
with love?

Winter Banner

Materials

Completed design on white Country Aida 7; matching thread
2½ yards of coordinating fabric; matching thread
1¼ yards of fleece
1¼ yards of fusible interfacing
2⅜ yards of large cording
16½" length of 1¼"-wide wooden closet rod
Two 1½" x 4½" wooden finials
Clear Varnish
Glue
Paintbrush

Directions

All seams are ¼".

1. Complete Steps 1–5 of Directions for Spring Banner on page 12, using varnish in place of paints.

Paternayan Persian Yarn
(used for sample)

Step 1: Cross-stitch (1 strand)

		Code	Color
I		716	Mustard-vy. lt.
+	◿	745	Tobacco-vy. lt.
☐		733	Honey Gold
ⰵ		731	Honey Gold-dk.
•		825	Tangerine-vy. lt.
–		864	Copper-lt.
U		863	Copper
•		844	Salmon-lt.
△	◿	843	Salmon
∴		842	Salmon-med.
✕	◿	850	Spice-vy. dk.
–	◿	236	Cool Gray
○	◿	506	Federal Blue-lt.
✕	◿	505	Federal Blue
I	◿	514	Old Blue-lt.
U		513	Old Blue
+	◿	511	Old Blue-dk.

		Code	Color
–	◿	664	Pine Green-lt.
△		663	Pine Green
◿		662	Pine Green-med.
▲	◿	661	Pine Green-dk.
○		723	Autumn Yellow
◎		872	Rust-med.
◿		871	Rust-dk.
●		441	Golden Brown-dk.
◇		440	Golden Brown-vy. dk.
☐		462	Beige Brown
✕	◿	461	Beige Brown-med.
•		256	Warm Gray
○	◿	201	Steel Gray-dk.
∴	◿	222	Charcoal
■	◿	220	Black

Step 2: Backstitch (1 strand)

898 Coffee Brown-vy. dk.
DMC Pearl Cotton #8

Winter Banner

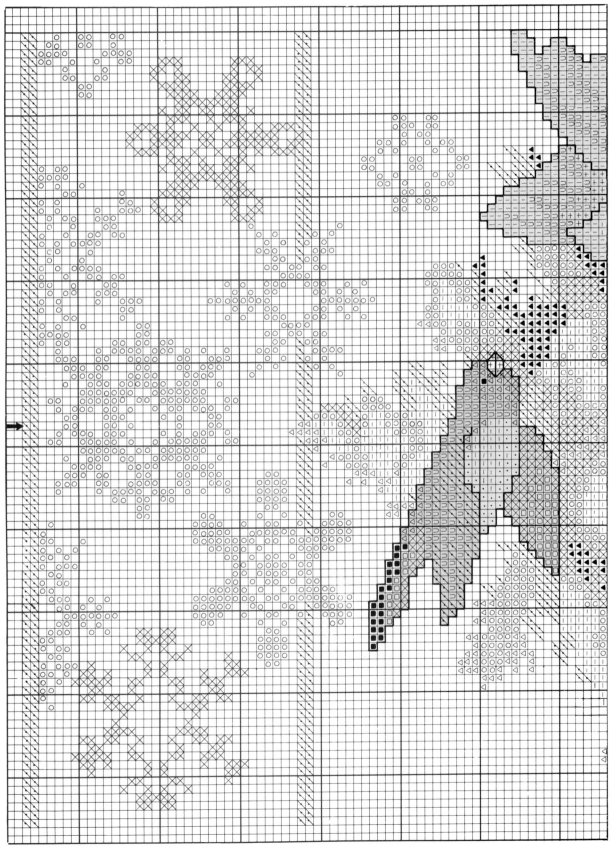

TOP

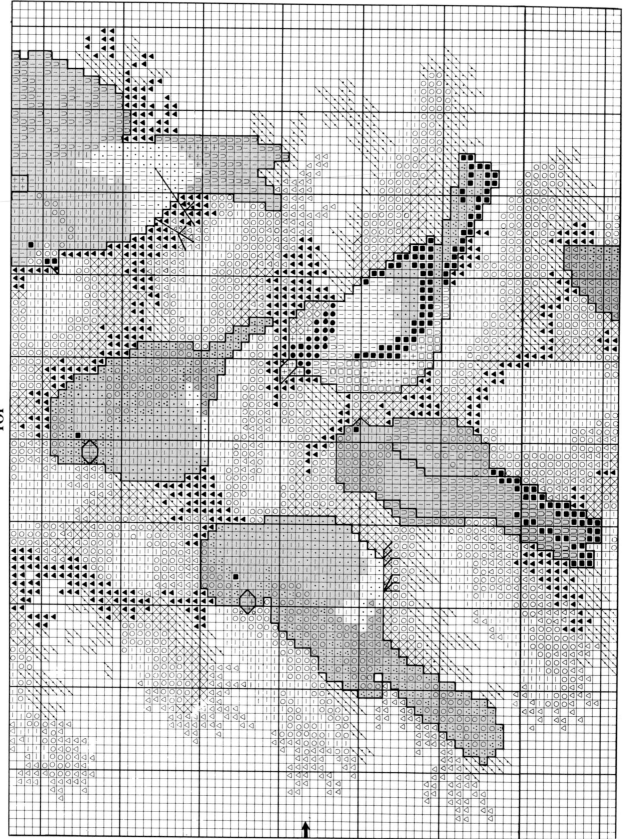

TOP

Winter Banner

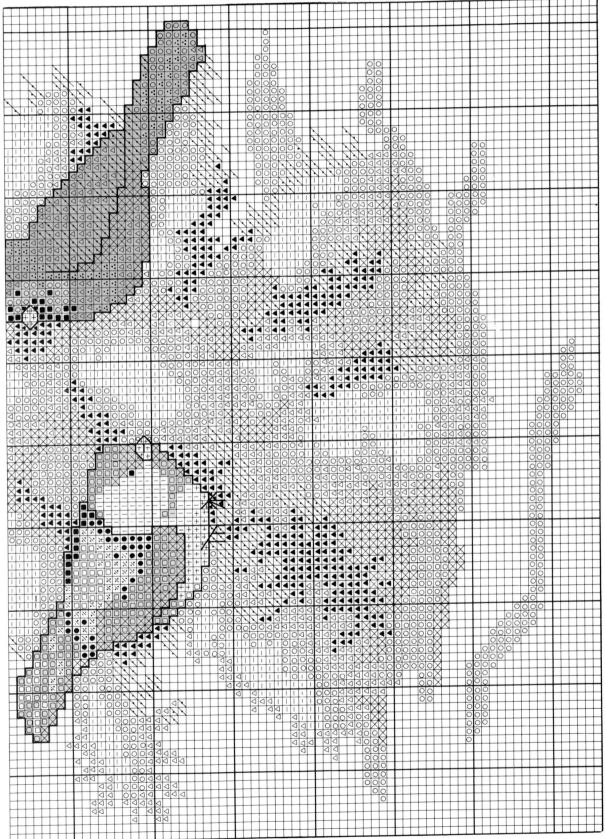

TOP

Stitch Count: 97 x 221

December Holiday

Stitched on white Linda 27 over two threads, the finished design size is 5¼" x 7¼". The fabric was cut 12" x 14". See March Charm on page 18 for cutout instructions.

December cutout

Anchor			DMC	(used for sample)
Step 1: Cross-stitch (2 strands)				
293	▲	◺	727	Topaz-vy. lt.
304	·		741	Tangerine-med.
271	⊠		3713	Salmon-vy. lt.
50	△		3716	Wild Rose-lt.
76	⊠		961	Wild Rose-dk.
13	○	◿	347	Salmon-vy. dk.
105	⊡		209	Lavender-dk.
101	●	◿	327	Antique Violet-vy. dk.
158	–	◿	775	Baby Blue-vy. lt.
167	–		519	Sky Blue
164	○		824	Blue-vy. dk.
206	·	◿	955	Nile Green-lt.
208	–	◿	563	Jade-lt.
210	⊠		562	Jade-med.
876	·		502	Blue Green
878	○		501	Blue Green-dk.
903	■		640	Beige Gray-vy. dk.
Step 2: Backstitch (1 strand)				
105			209	Lavender-dk. (line by numbers 1, 6)
164			824	Blue-vy. dk. (numbers)
879			500	Blue Green-vy. dk. (all else)

December Holiday

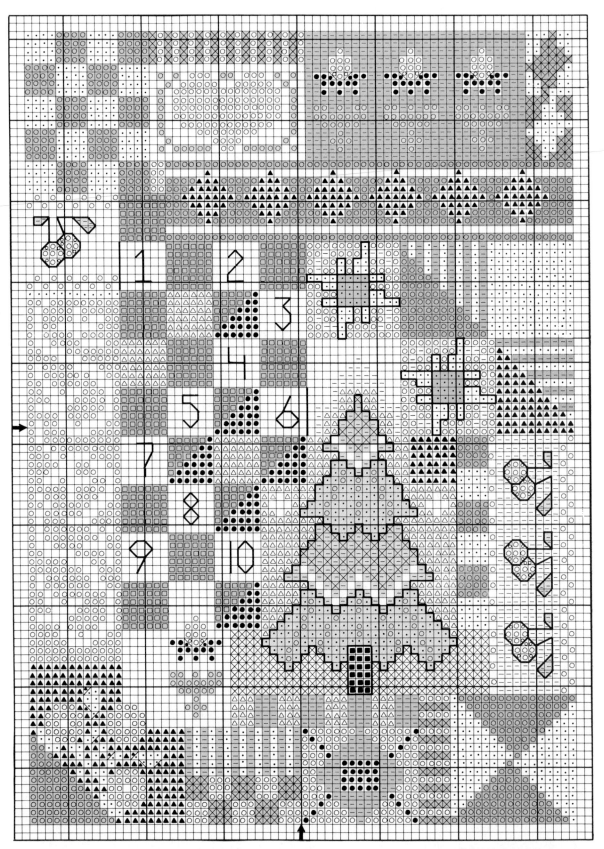

Stitch Count: 70 x 98

Holiday Runner

Holiday Runner

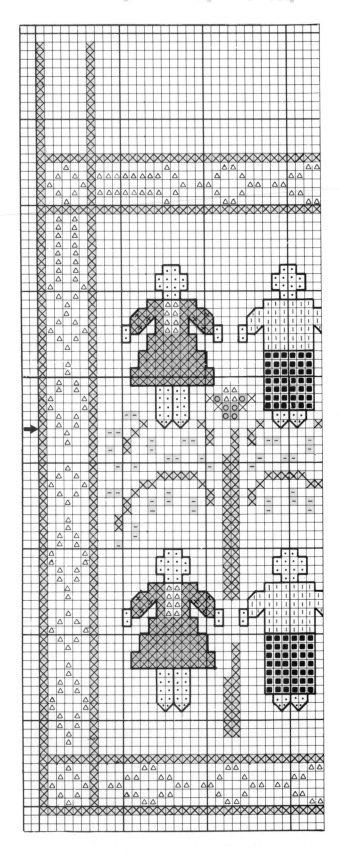

Stitched on driftwood Belfast Linen 32 over two threads, the finished design size is 11¼" x 5⅝". The fabric was cut 20" x 42½". Stitch design on each end of fabric, continuing vertical gray stitching the length of the fabric at intervals indicated on graph. For button hole stitch hem, mark 1¾" from each outside edge. Pull one thread; crease, folding to right side of fabric; hem. See Suppliers for specialty thread.

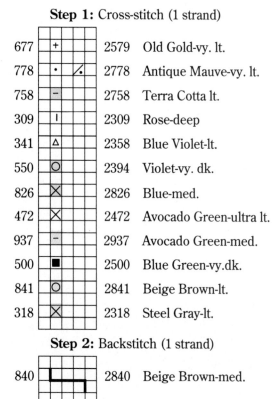

DMC Floss   **DMC Flower Thread (used for sample)**

Step 1: Cross-stitch (1 strand)

DMC Floss			DMC Flower Thread	
677	+		2579	Old Gold-vy. lt.
778	·	╱	2778	Antique Mauve-vy. lt.
758	–		2758	Terra Cotta lt.
309	❘		2309	Rose-deep
341	△		2358	Blue Violet-lt.
550	◯		2394	Violet-vy. dk.
826	✕		2826	Blue-med.
472	✕		2472	Avocado Green-ultra lt.
937	–		2937	Avocado Green-med.
500	■		2500	Blue Green-vy.dk.
841	◎		2841	Beige Brown-lt.
318	✕		2318	Steel Gray-lt.

Step 2: Backstitch (1 strand)

840	⌐	2840	Beige Brown-med.

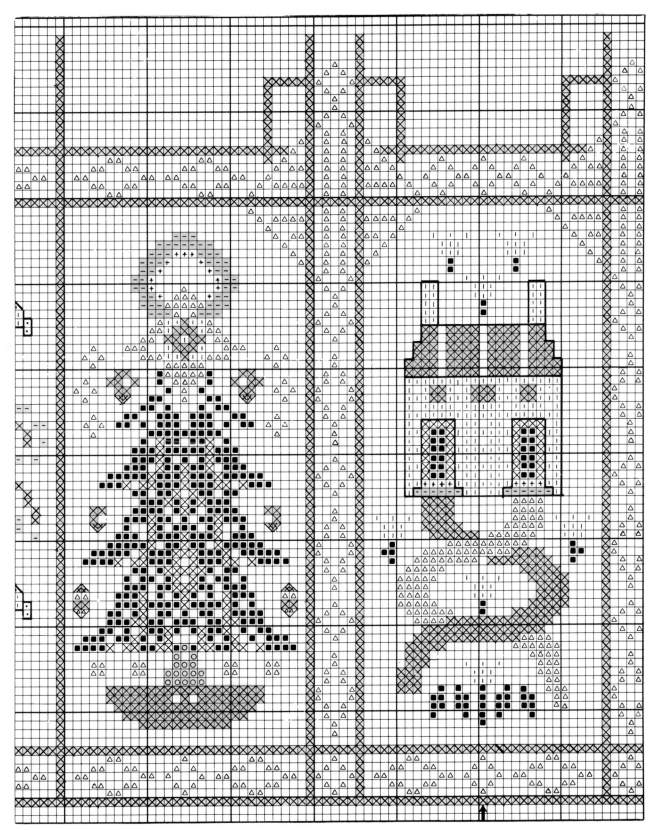

210
Holiday Runner

Stitch Count: 181 x 90

Crystal Snowflakes

Stitched on white Jobelan 28 over two threads, the finished design size is 3⅞" x 3⅞". The fabric was cut 6" x 6". More than one thread represented by a single symbol on the code and graph indicates blending; note the number of strands used. See Suppliers for specialty thread and fabric.

Materials
(for one coaster)

Completed design on white Jobelan 28
4" square of blue fabric for back; matching
  thread
4" square of fleece
1 skein of #809 Delft DMC floss
1 spool of #001 Silver Balger blending
  filament

Directions
All seams are ¼".

1. Trim design to 4" square (¼" outside last row of stitching) for front.

2. Pin fleece to wrong side of design piece. Stitch design piece to back with right sides facing and raw edges aligned, leaving an opening. Trim corners. Turn. Slipstitch opening closed.

3. For tassel, cut one 8" and one 5" piece each of floss and blending filament. Set aside.

4. Handling floss and blending filament as one, wrap 25 times around a 1½" card for each tassel. Using 5" floss and blending filament pieces, knot at top to secure. Cut threads at opposite end (**Diagram 1**).

Diagram 1

Using 8" floss and blending filament pieces, lay a narrow loop of yarn flat on tassel, looped end down and extending below area to be wrapped (**Diagram 2**). Wrap floss and filament over two strands that form loop. Then insert 2 through loop (**Diagram 3**). Pull up on 1 to secure loop and thread inside neck (**Diagram 4**). Cut off ends. Make four tassels, attaching one to each coaster corner.

Diagram 2   Diagram 3   Diagram 4

213
Crystal Snowflakes

Stitch Count: 54 x 54

Anchor   **DMC (used for sample)**

Step 1: Cross-stitch (2 strands)

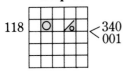

118 <340 Blue Violet-med. (1 strand)+
     <001 Silver Balger blending
           filament (1 strand)

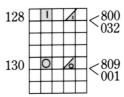

128 <800 Delft-pale (1 strand)+
     <032 Pearl Balger blending
           filament (1 strand)

130 <809 Delft (1 strand)+
     <001 Silver Balger blending
           filament (1 strand)

Christmas Plaid

Blue Plaid Stocking

Stitched on raw linen Belfast Linen 32 over two threads, the finished design size is 7" x 8¼". The fabric was cut 13" x 15". More than one thread represented by a single symbol on the code and graph indicates blending; note the number of strands used. See Suppliers for specialty thread and buttons.

Red Plaid Stocking

Stitched on raw linen Belfast Linen 32 over two threads, the finished design size is 6" x 8⅛". The fabric was cut 12" x 15". More than one thread represented by a single symbol on the code and graph indicates blending; note the number of strands used. See Suppliers for specialty thread and buttons.

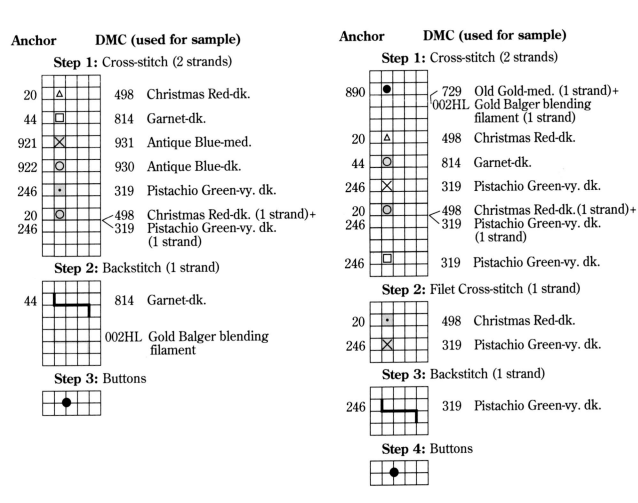

Anchor   **DMC (used for sample)**

Step 1: Cross-stitch (2 strands)

Anchor		DMC	
20	△	498	Christmas Red-dk.
44	□	814	Garnet-dk.
921	⊠	931	Antique Blue-med.
922	○	930	Antique Blue-dk.
246	·	319	Pistachio Green-vy. dk.
20 / 246	○	498 / 319	Christmas Red-dk. (1 strand) + Pistachio Green-vy. dk. (1 strand)

Step 2: Backstitch (1 strand)

44	⌐	814	Garnet-dk.
		002HL	Gold Balger blending filament

Step 3: Buttons

Anchor   **DMC (used for sample)**

Step 1: Cross-stitch (2 strands)

Anchor		DMC	
890	●	729 / 002HL	Old Gold-med. (1 strand) + Gold Balger blending filament (1 strand)
20	△	498	Christmas Red-dk.
44	○	814	Garnet-dk.
246	⊠	319	Pistachio Green-vy. dk.
20 / 246	○	498 / 319	Christmas Red-dk. (1 strand) + Pistachio Green-vy. dk. (1 strand)
246	□	319	Pistachio Green-vy. dk.

Step 2: Filet Cross-stitch (1 strand)

20	·	498	Christmas Red-dk.
246	⊠	319	Pistachio Green-vy. dk.

Step 3: Backstitch (1 strand)

246	⌐	319	Pistachio Green-vy. dk.

Step 4: Buttons

Christmas Plaid

Materials
(for one stocking)

Completed design on raw linen Belfast
   Linen 32
½ yard of unstitched raw linen Belfast
   Linen 32
1 yard of delft blue fabric; matching thread
1¼ yard of small cording
⅛ yard of fleece
Tracing paper
Dressmaker's pen
Ceramic buttons (optional)

Directions
All seams are ¼".
(for one stocking)

1. Using stocking pattern on graph, mark
outline on design piece, adding seam
allowance. Cut out. From unstitched linen,
cut one stocking piece for back. From fleece,
cut two stocking pieces. From blue fabric,
cut two stocking pieces for lining and a 1" x
3" strip for hanger. Also, cut 1"-wide bias
strips, piecing as needed to equal 1¼ yards.
Make corded piping and cut into a 28" and a
10½" length.

Christmas Plaid

2. With right sides facing, fold hanger strip in half lengthwise. Stitch long edge to make a tube. Turn right side out. Position seam in center back and press. Fold hanger in half with raw edges aligned.

3. Pin fleece to wrong side of stocking front. Repeat with stocking back. With right sides facing and raw edges aligned, stitch 28" length of piping around sides and bottom of stocking front. With right sides facing, stitch stocking front to stocking back, sewing on piping stitching line and leaving top open. Trim fleece from seam allowance. Clip curves. Turn. Repeat with remaining piping around top of stocking.

4. For lining, stitch front to back with right sides facing and raw edges aligned, leaving top edge open and a large opening in side seam above heel. Clip curves. Do not turn. With right sides facing, slide lining over stocking, matching side seams. With top raw edges aligned, sandwich hanger between lining and piping in the top right-hand edge of stocking back. Sew lining to stocking on piping stitching line, catching hanger in seam. Turn stocking through opening in lining. Slipstitch opening closed. Tuck lining inside stocking.

Christmas Plaid

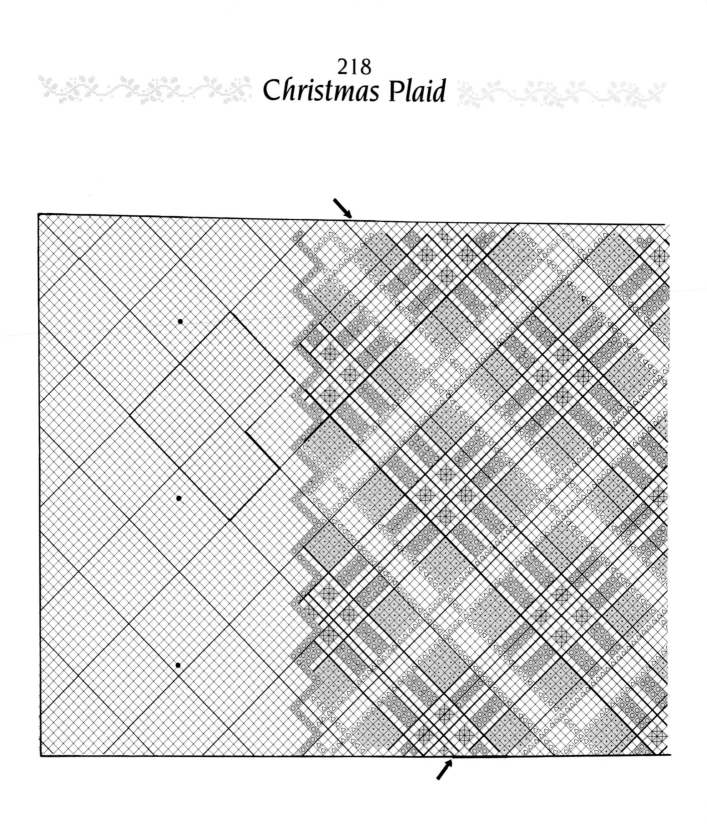

Christmas Plaid

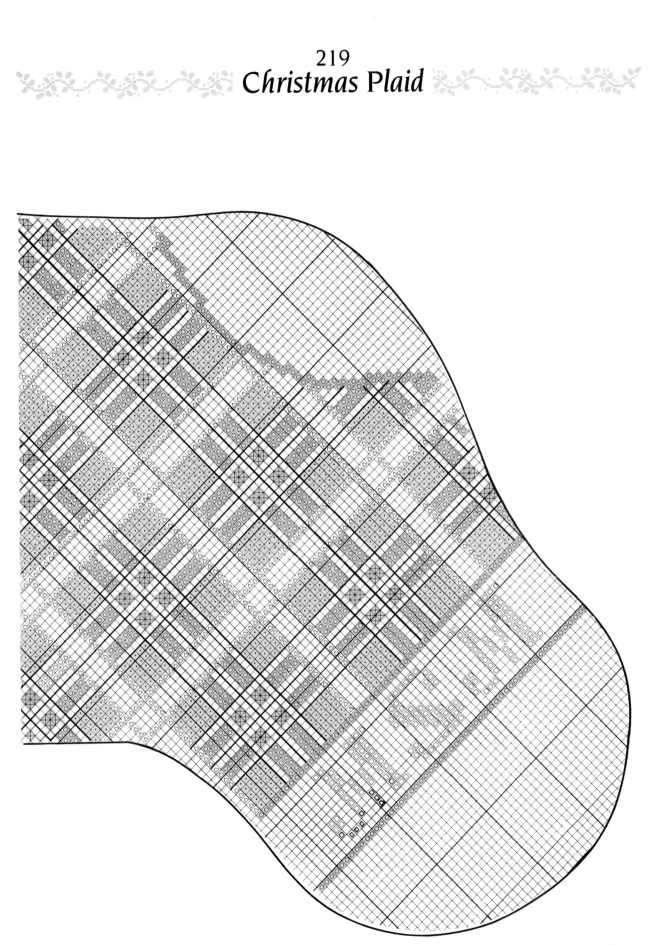

Stitch Count: 112 x 132 (Blue plaid stocking)

Christmas Plaid

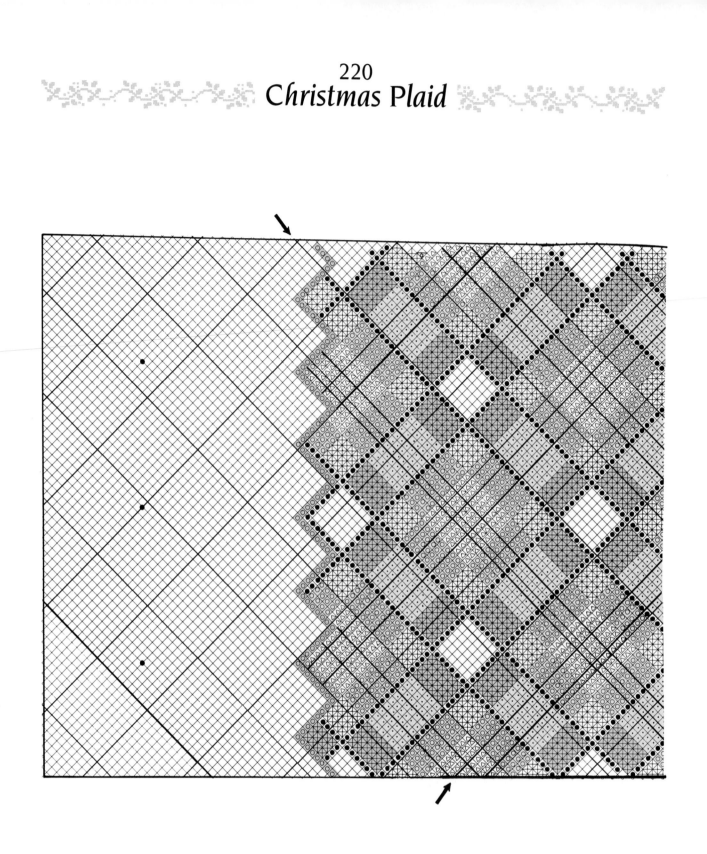

221
Christmas Plaid

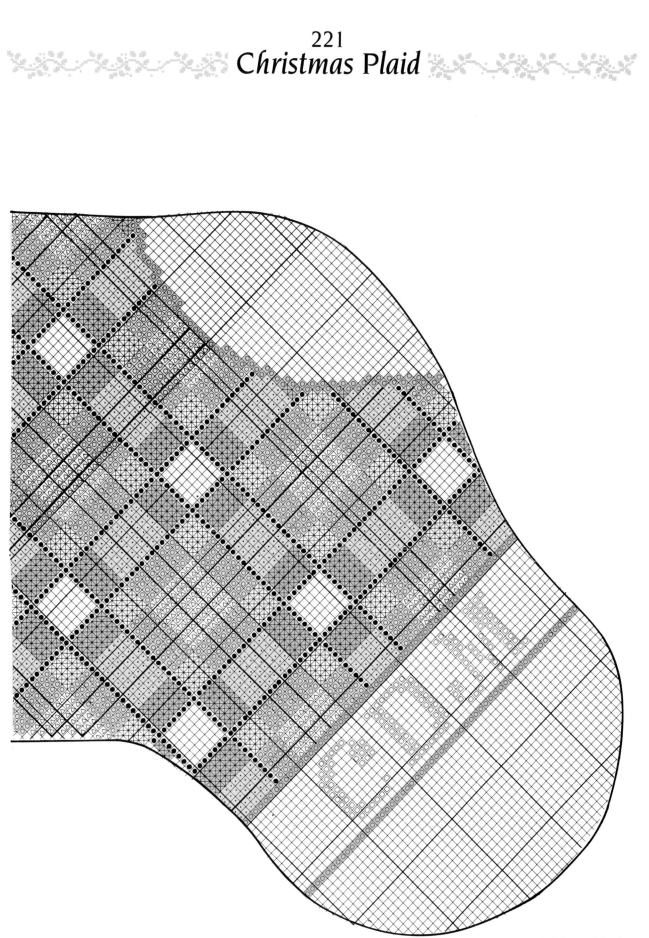

Stitch Count: 96 x 130 (Red plaid stocking)

Apricot Stocking

Stitched on apricot Pastel Linen 28 over two threads, the finished design size is 1¼" x 3⅜" for each motif. The fabric was cut 20" x 12". Heavy lines on graph indicate repeats. Repeat motif across 15½". Stitch only on fabric that can be worked over two threads. See Suppliers for specialty thread.

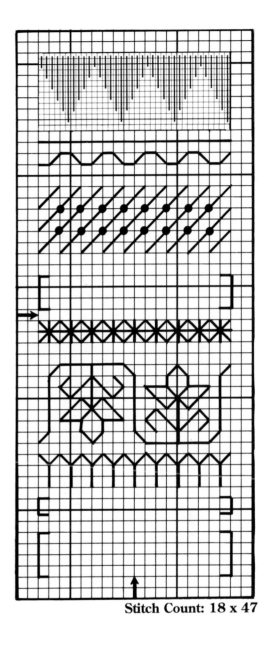

Stitch Count: 18 x 47

Anchor   **DMC (used for sample)**

Step 1: Long Stitch (2 strands)

8   353   Peach (Each repeat is over 6 horizontal and 10 vertical threads.)

Step 2: Backstitch (1 strand)

     021   Copper Balger blending filament

Step 3: Slanted Pulled Thread (2 strands)

271   761   Salmon-lt. (Work over 4 vertical and 4 horizontal threads, slightly pulling to create small holes at dots.)

Step 4: Serpentine Hemstitch (1 strand)

9   760   Salmon (Remove 6 horizontal threads. Hemstitch top and bottom edges in groups of 4 vertical threads.)

Step 5: Smyrna Cross (2 strands)

4146   754   Peach-lt.

Step 6: Backstitch (1 strand)

9   760   Salmon

Step 7: Fly Stitch (2 strands)

9   760   Salmon

Step 8: Vandyke Stitch (2 strands)

271   761   Salmon-lt. (Stitch over 3 horizontal and 2 vertical threads.)

Step 9: Twisted Ladder Hemstitch (1 strand)

     021   Copper Balger blending filament (Needle weave with 2 strands. Remove 8 horizontal threads; hemstitch top and bottom edges in groups of 4 vertical threads; then twist.)

Materials

Completed design on apricot Pastel Linen 28
1 yard of peach silk; matching thread
4 yards of ⅝"-wide wired peach ribbon
3 yards of 1"-wide sheer silk peach ribbon
½ yard of fleece
1¼ yards of medium cording
Tracing paper
Dressmaker's pen

Directions
All seams are ¼".

1. Trim design piece to 15½" x 7½" for cuff. Allow ½" of unstitched linen above top row of stitching. Make patterns; see page 225.

2. From silk, cut four stockings, two soles, one 2½" x 5" piece for hanger, four 16" x 3" pieces for large roses, three 10" x 3" pieces for medium roses and three 5" x 3" pieces for buds. Also from silk, cut 1¾"-wide bias strips, piecing as needed to equal 1¼ yards. Make 1¼ yards of corded piping. Cut two stockings and one sole from fleece.

3. To make stocking, baste one fleece stocking to wrong side of one silk stocking for front. Repeat for back. With right sides facing, stitch stocking front to back, leaving bottom and top edges open. Trim fleece from seam allowances. Turn. With right sides facing, stitch remaining silk stockings for lining, leaving bottom and top edges open.

4. To make cuff, fold design piece in half with right sides facing and short edges aligned. Stitch short edge to make a tube. Turn. Fold with wrong sides facing and long raw edges aligned. Slide cuff over top of stocking with design side out and raw edges aligned. Baste to top edge of stocking. Stitch piping over cuff, aligning raw edges and securing all layers. Stitch piping to bottom edge of stocking.

5. With right sides facing and raw edges aligned, fold hanger in half lengthwise. Stitch long raw edge. Turn. With short raw edges aligned, fold in half; press. Pin hanger on heel side seam at top edge. Slide lining over stocking, right sides facing and top edges aligned. Stitch top edge on stitching line of piping. Fold lining inside stocking. Baste bottom edges through all layers. Turn wrong side out.

6. To complete stocking, layer one sole (right side down), fleece and remaining sole (right side up); baste. Stitch sole pieces to bottom edge of stocking, sewing on stitching line of piping. Turn right side out.

7. To make large rose, fold one silk piece with long edges aligned. Knot one end for center of rose. Fold and tack remaining fabric around center to complete rose (**Diagram 1**). Make three additional large roses and three medium roses in the same way. To make bud, fold and tack fabric (**Diagram 2**); make three buds. Center and tack large roses and buds over toe side seam as desired; see photo. Center and tack medium roses over heel side seam near hanger. Cut wired ribbon into two equal pieces. Loop and tack as desired around roses. Repeat with silk ribbon; see photo.

Apricot Stocking

Diagram 1

Diagram 2

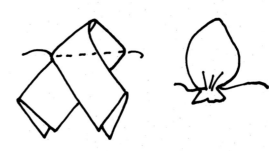

Each square equals 1"

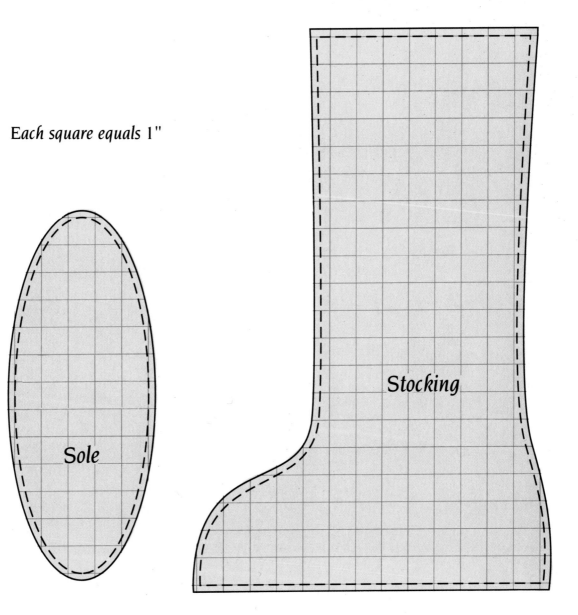

Sole

Stocking

January Wonder

Stitched on white Aida 14, the finished design size is 4⅞" x 6¾". The fabric was cut 11" x 13". See March Charm on page 18 for cutout instructions.

January cutout

Anchor			DMC (used for sample)	
Step 1: Cross-stitch (2 strands)				
1	•			White
295	+	⟋	726	Topaz-lt.
323	△	◸	722	Orange Spice-lt.
48	•		818	Baby Pink
50	–		3716	Wild Rose-lt.
76	□		961	Wild Rose-dk.
95	⁒	◹	554	Violet-lt.
158	○		775	Baby Blue-vy. lt.
159	–		3325	Baby Blue-lt.
154	U		3755	Baby Blue
147	⊠		312	Navy Blue-lt.
149	∴		311	Navy Blue-med.
185	⊠		964	Seagreen-lt.
186	∴		959	Seagreen-med.
203	–		564	Jade-vy. lt.
914	⟋		3772	Pecan-med.
403	●		310	Black
Step 2: Backstitch (1 strand)				
149			311	Navy Blue-med. (snowman)
403			310	Black (all else)
Step 3: French Knot (1 strand)				
403	●		310	Black

January Wonder

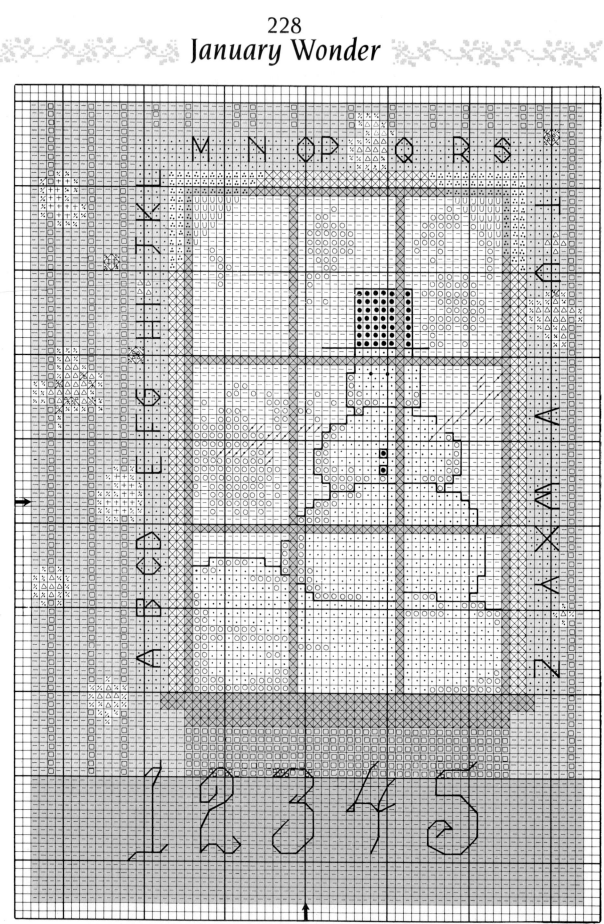

Stitch Count: 68 x 95

Winter Centerpiece

Winter Centerpiece

Stitched on oatmeal Floba 25 over two threads, the finished design size is 4⅜" x 2⅛" for each motif. See Step 1 of Directions before cutting and stitching fabric.

Materials

Two completed designs on oatmeal Floba 25; matching thread
Hurricane chimney

Directions

All seams are ¼".

1. Complete Steps 1–3 of Autumn Bands on page 187, substituting the chimney for the flowerpot and cutting two fabric strips instead of one.

2. Fold in seam allowance on one end of band. Wrap around chimney. Insert raw edge of other end into folded end. Slipstitch ends together. Repeat for remaining fabric strip.

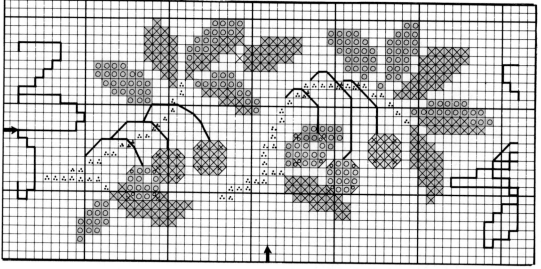

Stitch Count: 54 x 26 (each motif)

Anchor   DMC (used for sample)

Step 1: Cross-stitch (2 strands)

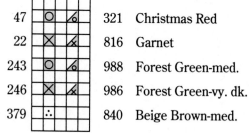

47	321	Christmas Red
22	816	Garnet
243	988	Forest Green-med.
246	986	Forest Green-vy. dk.
379	840	Beige Brown-med.

Step 2: Backstitch (1 strand)

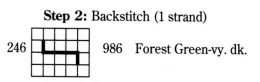

| 246 | 986 | Forest Green-vy. dk. |

Hide Away Boxes

Hide Away Boxes

Box 1 was stitched on white Dublin Linen 25 over two threads. The finished design size is 2⅝" x 2½" for lid and 1⅞" x 1½" for inside saying. The fabric was cut 7" x 7" for each. See Suppliers for specialty thread.

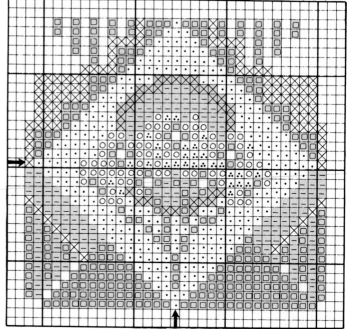

Stitch Count: 33 x 31 (Box Lid 1)

Materials
(for one box)

Two completed designs (box lid and inside
saying); matching thread
Wooden box (see Suppliers)
Acrylic paints
Paintbrushes
Sponges
Fleece
Mat board
Hot glue gun and glue

Directions
(for one box)
All seams are ¼".

1. Paint box with acrylic paints as desired. Allow to dry.

2. To complete model, zigzag outer edges of each design piece. Cut two fleece pieces and one mat board to match lid insert. Center and glue fleece, then lid design over lid insert; place in box lid. Repeat with fleece, saying and mat board. Insert inside lid, gluing design backs together.

DMC		Marlitt (used for sample)	
Step 1: Cross-stitch (2 strands)			
745	·	1013	Yellow-lt. pale.
948	–	1213	Peach-vy. lt.
761	✕	1019	Salmon-lt.
760	∴	830	Salmon
3712	O	831	Salmon-med.
210	✕	816	Lavender-med.
334	□	1009	Baby Blue-med.
772	–	1058	Pine Green-lt.
989	□	897	Forest Green
Step 2: Backstitch (1 strand)			
334		1009	Baby Blue-med. (lettering inside box)
Step 3: French Knot (1 strand)			
334	●	1009	Baby Blue-med.

Stitch Count: 23 x 19 (Saying 1)

Box 2 was stitched on cream Pastel Linen 28 over two threads. The finished design size is 6½" x 2½" for lid and 6¼" x 1¾" for inside saying. The fabric was cut 11" x 7" for each.

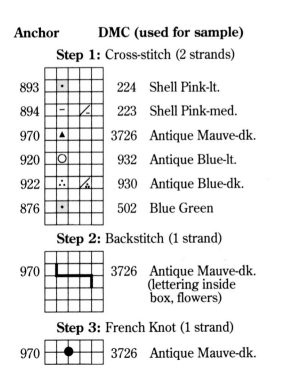

Anchor		DMC (used for sample)	

Step 1: Cross-stitch (2 strands)

893	·	224	Shell Pink-lt.
894	− ⁄	223	Shell Pink-med.
970	▲	3726	Antique Mauve-dk.
920	O	932	Antique Blue-lt.
922	∴ ⁄	930	Antique Blue-dk.
876	·	502	Blue Green

Step 2: Backstitch (1 strand)

970		3726	Antique Mauve-dk. (lettering inside box, flowers)

Step 3: French Knot (1 strand)

970	●	3726	Antique Mauve-dk.

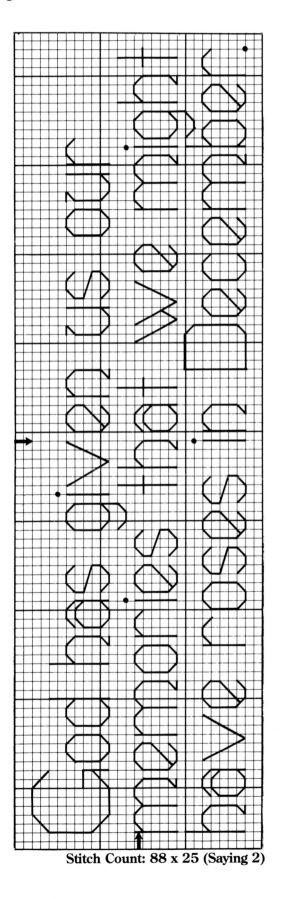

Stitch Count: 88 x 25 (Saying 2)

Hide Away Boxes

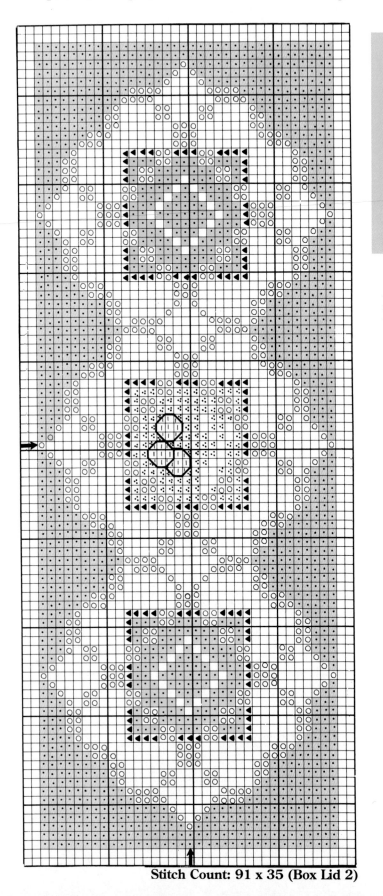

Stitch Count: 91 x 35 (Box Lid 2)

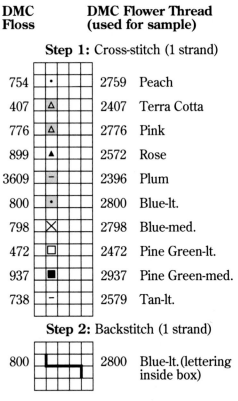

Box 3 was stitched on cream Murano 30 over two threads. The finished design size is 6⅛" x 2⅜" for lid and 6⅝" x 1½" for inside saying. The fabric was cut 11" x 7" for each. See Suppliers for specialty thread.

DMC Floss		DMC Flower Thread (used for sample)	

Step 1: Cross-stitch (1 strand)

754	·	2759	Peach
407	△	2407	Terra Cotta
776	▲	2776	Pink
899	▲	2572	Rose
3609	−	2396	Plum
800	·	2800	Blue-lt.
798	✕	2798	Blue-med.
472	□	2472	Pine Green-lt.
937	■	2937	Pine Green-med.
738	−	2579	Tan-lt.

Step 2: Backstitch (1 strand)

800		2800	Blue-lt. (lettering inside box)

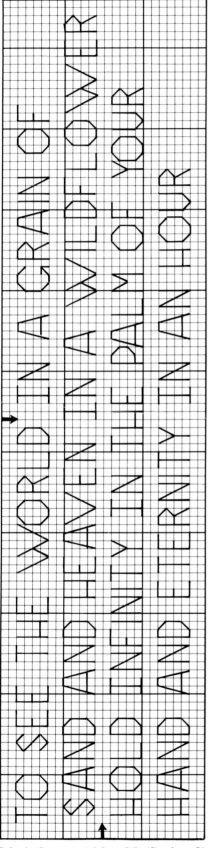

Stitch Count: 100 x 22 (Saying 3)

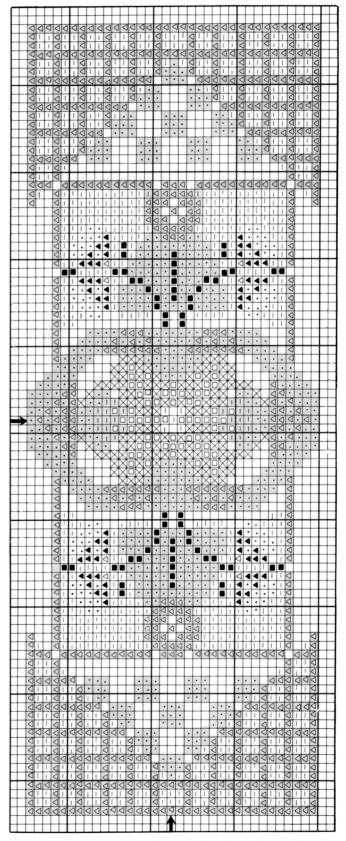

Stitch Count: 91 x 35 (Box Lid 3)

February Hearts

Stitched on white Jobelan 28 over two threads, the finished design size is 4⅞" x 7¼". The fabric was cut 11" x 13". More than one thread represented by a single symbol on the code and graph indicates blending; note the number of strands used. See March Charm on page 18 for cutout instructions.

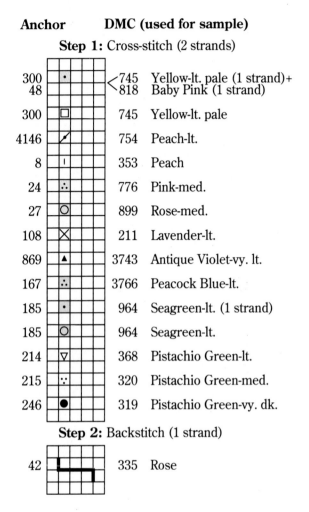

Anchor		DMC (used for sample)	

Step 1: Cross-stitch (2 strands)

Anchor		DMC	
300	·	745	Yellow-lt. pale (1 strand)+
48		818	Baby Pink (1 strand)
300	▢	745	Yellow-lt. pale
4146	╱	754	Peach-lt.
8	ı	353	Peach
24	∴	776	Pink-med.
27	○	899	Rose-med.
108	⊠	211	Lavender-lt.
869	▲	3743	Antique Violet-vy. lt.
167	∴	3766	Peacock Blue-lt.
185	•	964	Seagreen-lt. (1 strand)
185	○	964	Seagreen-lt.
214	▽	368	Pistachio Green-lt.
215	∷	320	Pistachio Green-med.
246	●	319	Pistachio Green-vy. dk.

Step 2: Backstitch (1 strand)

Anchor		DMC	
42	⌐	335	Rose

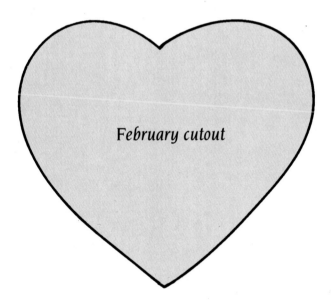

February cutout

February Hearts

Stitch Count: 69 x 101

Love Lights

Love Lights

Stitched on ash rose Murano 30 over two threads, the finished design size is 2⅛" x 2⅛" for each design. The fabric was cut 13" x 6½" for each. Cut and stitch four, centering each design.

Materials
(for one candle holder)

Four completed designs on ash rose
 Murano 30; matching thread
Four 2½" wooden cubes with 1"-diameter,
 1"-deep hole in center of each top
Rose acrylic paint
Sponge
Four 1"-diameter candle-cup inserts
2 yards each of ³⁄₁₆"-wide rose and lavender
 ribbon
2 yards of ¹⁄₁₆"-wide pink braid
Glue

Directions
All seams are ¼".

1. Paint top and bottom of each cube. Allow to dry. Place a candle-cup insert in hole of each cube.

2. Trim 1" from each short edge and ½" from each long edge of design piece. With right sides facing and long raw edges aligned, fold design piece in half. Stitch long edge to make a tube. Turn right side out. Position seam in center back and press.

3. Wrap band around cube. Fold in seam allowance on one short end of fabric. Insert raw edge of other end into folded end. Slipstitch ends together.

4. Cut ribbons and braid into 18" lengths. Take one length of each, and handling as one, tie a bow. Glue bow to top corner of candle holder; see photo. Repeat Steps 1–4 with remaining cubes and strips.

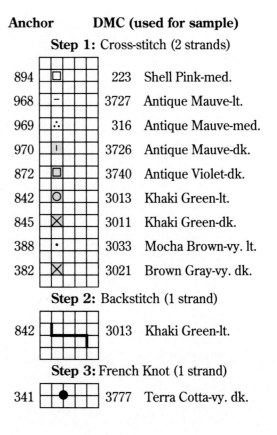

Anchor		DMC	(used for sample)
Step 1: Cross-stitch (2 strands)			
894	□	223	Shell Pink-med.
968	–	3727	Antique Mauve-lt.
969	∴	316	Antique Mauve-med.
970	I	3726	Antique Mauve-dk.
872	▣	3740	Antique Violet-dk.
842	○	3013	Khaki Green-lt.
845	✕	3011	Khaki Green-dk.
388	·	3033	Mocha Brown-vy. lt.
382	✕	3021	Brown Gray-vy. dk.
Step 2: Backstitch (1 strand)			
842	⌐	3013	Khaki Green-lt.
Step 3: French Knot (1 strand)			
341	●	3777	Terra Cotta-vy. dk.

Love Lights

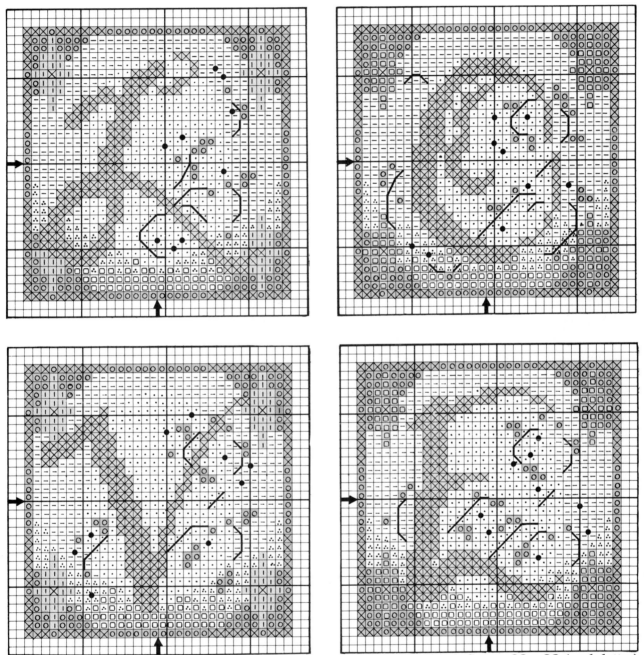

Stitch Count: 32 x 32 (each letter)

Valentine Tabletop

Stitched on cream Murano 30 over two threads, the finished design size is 8⅛" x 6¾". The fabric was cut 16" x 16".

Materials

Completed design on cream Murano 30
6" square of pink fabric; matching thread
Shaker table (see Suppliers)
White latex paint
Paintbrushes
Acrylic paints: pink, blue, yellow, green
Sponges
Fine sandpaper
Tracing paper
Manila folder for stencil patterns
Craft knife
Fleece
Hot glue gun and glue

Directions

All seams are ¼".

1. Paint table with a base coat of white latex paint. Then paint with acrylic paints as desired. Allow to dry. Sand surface lightly.

2. Trace heart pattern, transferring to pink fabric; cut out three hearts. To attach hearts to design piece, clip seam allowances of curved edges, folding to wrong side; press and baste. Place hearts right side up on right side of design piece as desired and slipstitch with close, small stitches, using matching thread.

3. Transfer stencil patterns to folder. Cut out patterns with a craft knife. Stencil flowers as desired to design piece. Let dry.

4. To complete model, cut fleece same size as tabletop insert. Glue to insert. Zigzag outer edges of design piece. Center over fleece and glue, inserting in tabletop.

Heart

Stencil

Valentine Tabletop

Anchor   **DMC (used for sample)**

Step 1: Cross-stitch (2 strands)

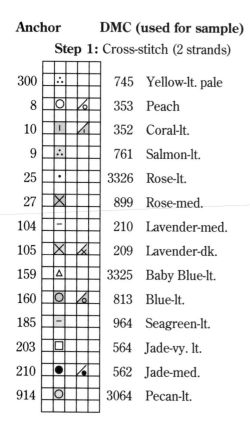

Anchor			DMC	
300			745	Yellow-lt. pale
8	○	◢	353	Peach
10	I	◿	352	Coral-lt.
9	∴		761	Salmon-lt.
25	•		3326	Rose-lt.
27	⊠		899	Rose-med.
104	−		210	Lavender-med.
105	⊠	◹	209	Lavender-dk.
159	△		3325	Baby Blue-lt.
160	○	◢	813	Blue-lt.
185	−		964	Seagreen-lt.
203	□		564	Jade-vy. lt.
210	●	◢	562	Jade-med.
914	○		3064	Pecan-lt.

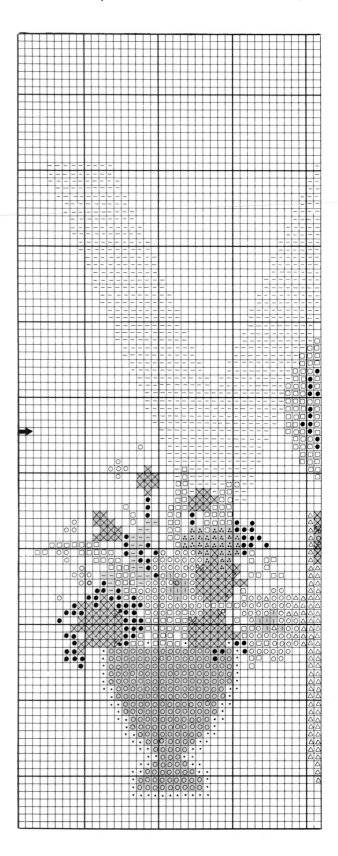

Valentine Tabletop

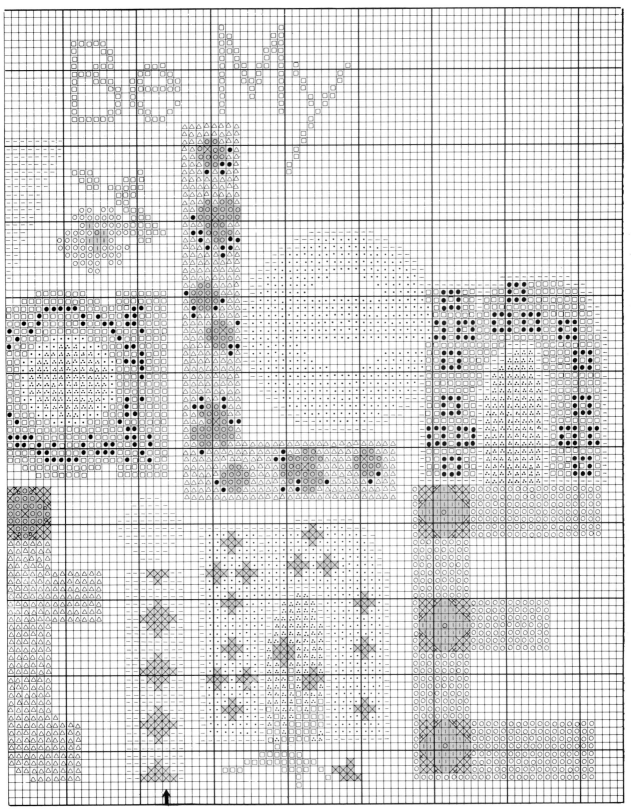

Stitch Count: 121 x 101

Romantic Pillow

Stitched on ash rose Murano 30 over two threads, the finished design size is 4½" x 3¾". The fabric was cut 7" x 7".

Materials

Completed design on ash rose Murano 30; matching thread

One 13½" x 15" piece of cream fabric; matching thread

⅛ yard of dark lavender fabric; matching thread

⅛ yard of medium lavender fabric; matching thread

⅛ yard of light lavender fabric; matching thread

Polyester stuffing

Scrap of fleece

2 yards of ¼"-wide dark lavender silk ribbon

2 yards of ¼"-wide medium lavender silk ribbon

2 yards of ¼"-wide light lavender silk ribbon

One 6"-long needle

Tracing paper

Directions
All seams are ¼".

1. Make 5½" x 5¼" heart pattern. Center over design piece; cut one. From fleece, cut one heart, trimming ¼" from edges. Make patterns for 8½"-wide circle and 4"-wide circle. From dark lavender fabric, cut six 4" circles. From medium lavender fabric, cut two 8½" circles and six 4" circles. From light lavender fabric, cut four 4" circles.

2. Baste fleece to wrong side of design piece. Center on cream fabric, designating one 13½" edge as the top. Fold under ¼" and slipstitch.

3. Zigzag both 15" edges of cream fabric. With right sides facing, stitch 13½" edges together. Sew running stitch in one 15" edge. Gather tightly; secure thread. Stuff pillow firmly. Sew running stitch in second 15" edge. Gather and secure.

4. To make yo-yos from lavender circles, fold under ¼" on edges. Sew with running stitch using matching thread close to folded edge. Gather tightly; secure thread. Fold flat with gathered edge in center of right side.

5. Center large yo-yos over ends of pillow. Slipstitch. Place small yo-yos ½" from ends of pillow, alternating colors. Slipstitch. Using four strands of thread and long needle, secure thread in center of one large end yo-yo. Feed needle through pillow to opposite end and pull tightly; secure.

6. Cut ribbons into twelve 18" pieces. Handling two of each color as one, tie into bow. Trim ends. Repeat. Tack to centers of large end yo-yo.

248
Romantic Pillow

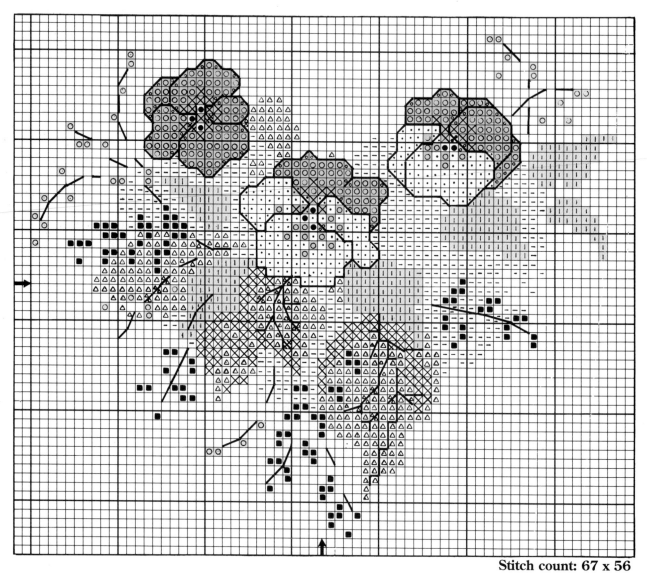

Stitch count: 67 x 56

Anchor   **DMC (used for sample)**

Step 1: Cross-stitch (2 strands)

386	.	∕.	746	Off White
891	●		676	Old Gold-lt.
4146	−	∕	950	Peach Pecan-dk.
896	◯		3722	Shell Pink
871	◯	∕	3041	Antique Violet-med.
872	✕		3740	Antique Violet-dk.
214	ǀ	∕	368	Pistachio Green-lt.

213	△	⊿	504	Blue Green-lt.
876	✕		502	Blue Green
878	■		501	Blue Green-dk.

Step 2: Backstitch (1 strand)

| 401 | | 844 | Beaver Gray-ultra dk. |

General Instructions

Easy Reference Features

Photo: The photograph, which is meant to be inspirational as well as instructional, shows the model(s) exactly as the design is presented in the cross-stitch graph and directions for completion.

Sample Paragraph: For every design, the sample paragraph identifies three features about the model: the fabric from which the model in the photo is stitched, the finished measurements of the design itself and the size to cut the fabric for finishing the design as it is shown in the photo. Any details unique to the model are also noted here.

Code: The code indicates the brand of the thread used in stitching the model as well as the cross-reference for using another brand. If the model is stitched in embroidery floss, which is most common, DMC brand is used for the model in the photo and Anchor is the cross-reference. If another product is used to stitch the model, the cross-reference is DMC embroidery floss. However, designs stitched in Paternayan Persian Yarn are not cross-referenced.

The steps in the code identify the stitch, such as cross-stitch, backstitch or beadwork, to be used and the number of floss strands for that stitch. Within the grid for each step are the symbols, which match the graph, with the color number and the color name for the thread. In some cases, a symbol sits under a diagonal line in the grid; this matches a symbol on the graph and indicates a half cross-stitch.

Blending: To achieve a unique effect, two threads are sometimes blended and stitched into the design as if they were one. Blended threads are represented on the graph and code with a single symbol. In the color names list, both threads are listed and the number of strands to be used is indicated.

Graph: Most of the cross-stitching "story" is told in the graph. Make one stitch for every symbol on the graph. Every different symbol represents another color. Refer to the code to verify which stitch to use. The small arrows in the left and bottom margins mark the center width and length of the design. Follow the marked grids from each edge to find the center. Match the center of the graph to the center of the fabric; begin stitching all designs in the center unless indicated otherwise in the sample paragraph.

For each of the products in the code, one unit is enough to complete the project; any exceptions are noted. For example, one skein of floss in each color or one tube of beads is enough for the project.

Below the lower right-hand corner of each graph is the stitch count, listing first the width, then the length of the design.

Materials: Beginning with the cross-stitched design, the materials list identifies the items used and the quantity needed to finish the model. Any special materials needed to finish a project, such as a wooden box, are listed under Suppliers, page 256.

Directions: In projects that require sewing, note the seam allowance. The directions offer step-by-step guidance for completing the model to match the one in the photograph. No finishing instructions are given for framed designs unless something unique has been done. It is expected that you will work with a professional framer who is experienced in stretching needlework to complete your projects.

Cross-stitch Guidelines

Fabrics: Counted cross-stitch is usually worked on even-weave fabric. Such fabric is manufactured specifically for counted thread embroidery, of which cross-stitch is the most familiar. This fabric is woven with the same number of vertical and horizontal threads per inch. Because the number of threads in the fabric is equal in each direction, each finished stitch is the same size. The number of threads per inch in even-weave fabrics determines the finished size of the design. In this book, projects are also worked on waste canvas and plastic canvas; see below.

Waste Canvas: Waste canvas is a coarse, fabric-like substance intended to provide a guide for cross-stitching on fabrics other than even-weaves. It allows for cross-stitch to be worked on everything from cotton broadcloth to sweatshirts. Cut the waste canvas 1" larger on all sides than the finished design size. Center and baste the canvas to the fabric being stitched. Complete all stitching. Then dampen the stitched area with cold water to remove the sizing in the canvas. Using tweezers, pull the waste canvas threads out one at a time. It is easier to remove all the threads in one direction first, then to remove the opposite threads. Allow the stitching to dry. Place design face side down on towel and iron it.

Plastic Canvas: Stitching on plastic canvas is similar to stitching on fabric; however, the graph and color code will look different. For plastic canvas, the symbols are placed on the intersections of the grid instead of inside the grid squares. While the stitches themselves are the same as on fabric, you will be counting meshes (the intersections) instead of holes. When the stitching is complete, carefully cut in the space between the bar of last row of stitching and next row of unstitched canvas. Then trim the nubs left from cutting between bars to achieve a smooth edge. After a plastic canvas design has been stitched and cut out, the edges are often finished by overcasting with evenly spaced, slanted diagonal stitches. The overcast stitch is also used to join two or more plastic canvas pieces. Simply align raw edges at the angle needed to complete the project and work the stitch through both pieces of plastic canvas.

Overcast Stitch

Other Fabrics: If you choose, use an even-weave fabric other than the one specified in the sample paragraph. To do this, you will need to recalculate the size of the finished design. Divide the width and the length of the stitch count by the number of threads per inch of the fabric you want to use. For example, a model stitched on Aida 14 has 14 threads per inch. To stitch the same design on Aida 11, divide both the width and the length of the stitch count by 11 for the adjusted finished design size.

When using fabrics with a small stitch count, you will be directed to stitch over two threads. In that case, every cross-stitch covers two threads across as well as two threads down. To calculate the stitch count for these designs, divide the thread count in half and use that number to divide into the stitch count. For example, Linda 28 over two threads is 14 stitches per inch. To calculate the finished design size, divide 14 into the width and length of the stitch count.

Convert a framed design to another fabric easily, using the formulas given above. Keep in mind that all projects with directions for finishing, such as pillows or banners, are based upon measurements for a fabric with the same stitch count as is specified in the sample paragraph. If you change fabrics, you will need to recalculate yardages and dimensions for the finished project.

Preparing Fabric: Cut even-weave fabric at least 3" larger on all sides than the finished design size, or cut it the size specified in the instructions. A 3" margin is the minimum amount of space to allow for working the edge of the design comfortably. To finish the item into a pillow, for example, the fabric should be cut as directed. To keep fabric from fraying, whipstitch, machine zigzag or over lock raw edges for a clean finish.

Needles: Needles should slip easily through the holes in the fabric, but not pierce the fabric. Use a blunt tapestry needle, size 24 or 26. Never leave the needle in the design area of work when you set aside your project. It can leave rust or a permanent impression on the fabric.

Floss: All numbers and color names are cross-referenced between Anchor and DMC brands of floss. Cut floss into 18" lengths; longer pieces tend to twist and knot. Run the floss over a damp sponge to straighten. Floss will cover best when lying flat. Separate all six strands and use the number of strands called for in the code. If floss is twisted, drop the needle and allow the floss to unwind itself.

Centering the Design: Find the center of the fabric by folding it in half horizontally and then vertically. Place a pin in the fold point to mark the center. Locate the center of the design on the graph by following the vertical and horizontal arrows. Begin stitching at the center point of the graph and the fabric.

Securing the Floss: Start by inserting your needle up from the underside of the fabric at your starting point. Hold 1" of thread behind the fabric and stitch over it, securing with the first few stitches. To finish thread, run under four or more stitches on the back of the design. Never knot floss unless working on clothing.

Stitching: For a smooth cross-stitch, use the "push and pull" method. Push the needle straight down and completely through fabric before pulling. Do not pull the thread tight. The tension should be consistent throughout, making the stitches even. Make one stitch for every symbol on the chart. To stitch in rows, work from left to right and then back. Half-crosses are used to make a rounded shape. Make the longer stitch in the direction of the slanted line.

Carrying Floss: To carry floss, weave floss under the previously worked stitches on the back. Do not carry your thread across any fabric that is not or will not be stitched. Loose threads, especially dark ones, will show through the fabric.

Cleaning Completed Work: When stitching is complete, soak it in cold water with a mild soap for 5–10 minutes. Rinse and roll in a towel to remove excess water; do not wring. Place work face down on a dry towel and iron on a warm setting until dry.

Stitches

Cross-stitch: Bring needle and thread up at 1, down at 2, up at 3, and down again at 4. For rows, stitch from left to right, then back. All stitches should lie in the same direction.

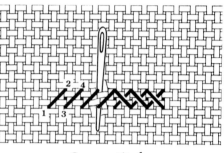

Cross-stitch

Filet Cross-stitch: Stitch the same as cross-stitch above, using only one strand of thread.

Half Cross-stitch: Make the longer stitch in the direction of the slanted line on the graph. The stitch actually fits three-fourths of the area. Bring the needle and thread up at 1, down at 2, up at 3 and down at 4.

Half Cross-stitch

Backstitch: Complete all cross-stitching before working backstitches or other accent stitches. Working from left to right with one strand of floss (unless otherwise designated on code), bring needle and thread up at 1, down at 2, and up again at 3. Go back at 1 and continue in this manner.

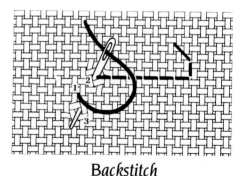

Backstitch

French Knot: Bring the needle and thread up at 1, using one strand of embroidery floss. Wrap floss around needle two times (unless otherwise indicated in instructions). Insert needle beside 1, pulling floss until it fits snugly around needle. Pull needle through to back.

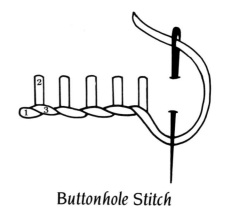

Buttonhole Stitch

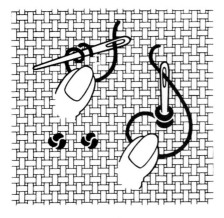

French Knot

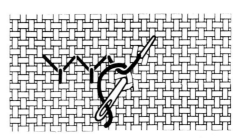

Fly Stitch

Beadwork: Attach beads to fabric stitching from lower left to upper right. Secure beads by returning thread through beads, lower right to upper left.

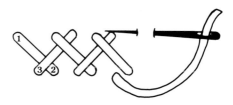

Herringbone Stitch

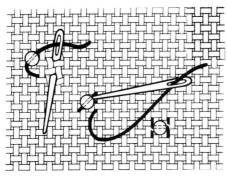

Beadwork

Lazy Daisy Stitch

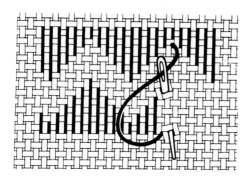

Long Stitch

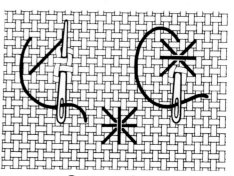

Smyrna Cross

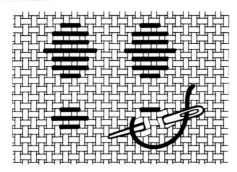

Satin Stitch

Twisted Ladder Hemstitch

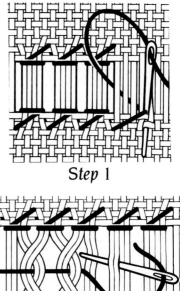

Step 1

Step 2

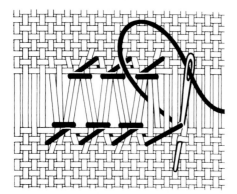

Serpentine Hemstitch

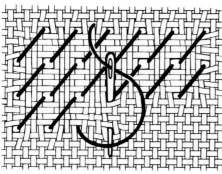

Slanted Pulled Thread

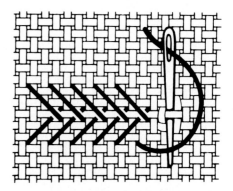

Vandyke Stitch

Sewing Guidelines

Patterns: Use tracing paper or template plastic to trace the patterns. Be sure to transfer all information. All patterns include seam allowances. The seam allowance is ¼" unless otherwise specified.

Marking on Fabric: Always use a dressmaker's pen or chalk to mark on fabric. It will wash out when you clean your finished piece.

Mitering Corners: Mitering adds a crisp, professional finish to corners on borders and bindings. Mitered borders have diagonal seams in the corner. To miter a corner, sew border strips up to, but not through, the seam allowance; backstitch. Repeat the process on all fours edges, making stitching lines meet exactly at the corners. Fold two adjacent border pieces together as shown in the diagram. Mark, then sew at a 45° angle. Trim the seam allowance to ¼" .

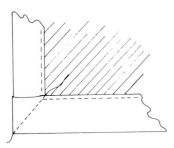

Mitered Corner

To miter a binding, stitch the bias to the project with right sides facing and using the seam allowance indicated. Stitch to, but not

through, the seam allowance; backstitch. Fold bias at a 90° angle to stitched edge and turn the corner. Resume stitching, meeting the backstitch at the seam allowance. Repeat at each corner. Fold bias to back, turning under seam allowance. Slipstitch, covering stitching line of binding and mitering each corner on both sides.

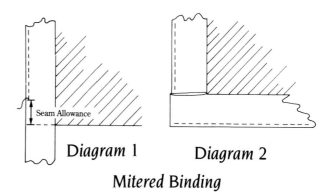

Diagram 1   *Diagram 2*
Mitered Binding

Narrow Hem: To hide a raw edge on a binding or the edge of a project, the directions will tell you to fold the fabric double to the wrong side. This means to fold ¼" of fabric along the edge to the wrong side, then fold the folded edge again. The directions will specify the width.

Corded Piping: Piece bias strips together to equal the requred length. Place the cording in the center of the wrong side of the bias strip and fold the bias strip over it, aligning raw edges. Using a zipper foot, stitch close to the cording through both layers of fabric. Trim the seam allowance to ¼".

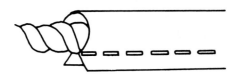

Corded Piping

Suppliers

The following businesses were of valuable assistance in the preparation of this book. For a merchant near you, write to the suppliers below.

Batting, fleece, polyester stuffing: Fairfield Processing Corporation, 88 Rose Hill Avenue, P.O. Drawer 1157, Danbury CT O6810

Beads: Mill Hill division of Gay Bowles Sales, Inc., P. O. Box 1060, Janesville WI 53547

DMC FLower Thread, Médicis Wool, Pearl Cotton #3, #5, #8: The DMC Corporation, Port Kearny Building #10, South Kearny NJ 07032-0650

Footstool (Aunt Mary's Footstool): Freeman Manufacturing, Inc., P. O. Box 362, Thomasville NC 27361-0362

Framing: Rett Ashby's Artist Touch, 5360 South 1900 West, Roy UT 84067

Hand-painted buttons (Christmas Plaid): Albe Creations Inc., 2920 Century Square, Winston-Salem NC 27106-2208

Hinged oak boxes (Hide Away Boxes)—044W (square), P48C (rectangle): Reed Baxter Woodcrafts Inc., P. O. Box 2186, Eugene OR 97402

Marlitt: Joan Toggitt Ltd., Weston Canal Plaza, 35 Fairfield Place, West Caldwell NJ 07006

Letter box (Daddy's Girl): Freeman Manufacturing, Inc., P. O. Box 362, Thomasville NC 27361-0362

Metallic Balger Blending Filament, Metallic Cord: Kreinik Mfg. Co., Inc., P. O. Box 1966, Parkersburg WV 26101

Paternayan Persian Yarn: Johnson Creative Arts, Inc., West Townsend MA 01474

Raised panel chest (Grandma's Sewing Box): Plain 'n' Fancy, P. O. Box 357, Mathews VA 2310

Sewing machine: Bernina of America, 534 W. Chestnut, Hinsdale IL 60521

Silk ribbon: YLI Corp., 482 N. Freedom Blvd., Provo UT 84601

Shaker table #47601 (Valentine Tabletop): Sudberry House, Box 895, Old Lyme CT 06371

Wood Mirror Frames: Chapelle Designers, P. O. Box 9252, Newgate Station, Ogden UT 84409

Wooden box (Treat Box): Zim's, P. O. Box 57620, Salt Lake City UT 84157

Fabric Suppliers: Zweigart/Joan Toggitt Ltd., Weston Canal Plaza, 35 Fairfield Place, West Caldwell NJ 07006

Cream Country Aida 7	Khaki Linda 27
White Country Aida 7	White Linda 27
Bone Tula 10	Apricot Pastel Linda 28
Cream Aida 14	Cream Pastel Linen 28
White Aida 14	Pistachio Pastel Linda 28
Daffodil Damask Aida 14	Amaretto Murano 30
Needlepoint Canvas 14	Ash Rose Murano 30
Rustico 14	Cream Murano 30
Waste Canvas 14	Moss Green Murano 30
Daffodil Damask Aida 18	Pewter Murano 30
Cream Hardanger 22	Wedgwood Murano 30
Sand Dublin Linen 25	Cream Belfast Linen 32
White Dublin Linen 25	Driftwood Belfast Linen 32
Floba 25	Raw Linen Belfast Linen 32
Celery Linda 27	

Chapelle Designers, P. O. Box 9252, Newgate Station, Ogden UT 84409
Vanessa-Ann Afghan Weave 18, Vanessa-Ann Damask 28

Charles Craft Inc., P.O. Box 1049, Laurinburg NC 28352
Wisteria Aida 14

Darice Incorporated, 21160 Drake Road, Strongsville OH 44136
Clear Plastic Canvas 7

Anne Powell Ltd., P. O. Box 3060, Stuart FL 34995
Glenshee Egyptian Cotton Quality D26

Wichelt, Rural Route #1, Stoddard WI 54658
White Jobelan 28